W.T.GRAHAM

GREATER
MANCHESTER

GREATER
MANCHESTER

125 Years
Images from the Manchester Evening News

The Breedon Books
Publishing Company
Derby

Publisher

First published in Great Britain by The Breedon Books Publishing Company Limited, 44 Friar Gate, Derby DE1 1DA.
1993.

Copyright

Manchester Evening News, 1993

Manchester Evening News Production Team

Compiled by Pam Garside with Lesley Breen.
Ted Stansfield, Richard Howarth and the Colour Process Department for all photographic reproduction.
Stan Roe, Raymond Coupes, Peter Matthews, Terry Hefferan and Paul Bayley for format, text and print advice.

Acknowledgements

We would like to thank the following people for their invaluable contributions towards this book.
Bobby Charlton CBE, for kindly agreeing to write the foreword.
Editorial contributors:- Michael Unger, Neville Bolton, Paul Horrocks, David Meek, Tom Waghorn, George Dowson and Bob Corfield.
Kevin Lee for finished artwork for the cover.
Eric Graham and MEN photographers - past and present.
MEN Libraries staff for additional photographic help and resources.
MEN Darkroom staff.
Ben Mellon, Denis Thorpe, Don McPhee, Ann Boulton and Jenny Partington for their support.

We would particularly like to thank everyone in the Systems, Composing and Process departments for their uncomplaining, cheerful, professional help and contributions, without which, this project would not have been possible.

ISBN 1 873626 67 3
Printed and bound by The Hillman Printer, Frome.
Cover printed by BDC Printing Services Ltd of Derby

Contents

Foreword

By Bobby Charlton CBE

The Manchester Evening News has been part of my life for more years than I care to remember.

The paper came into my world of football when, as a young player down from Newcastle, I would anxiously scan its pages for some recognition of my early performances.

Later I am happy to say I figured more prominently from time to time, occasionally of course to my discomfort if the reporter felt I had not played as well as I knew I had!

Overall though I think the Evening News has portrayed not just football and Manchester United, but the entire city in a meaningful way, reflecting our lives and times.

This has been particularly true of late during our campaign to bring the Olympic Games to Manchester in the year 2000.

The fact that we failed takes nothing away from the great efforts of both the paper and the Olympic workers.

I wish this special book covering 125 years of a great newspaper every success. The life of Manchester shines through its pages and I am delighted that medical research will benefit.

Introduction

This 1930s picture, by Manchester Guardian and Evening News photographer Tom Stuttard, illustrates our curiosity to know what is going on, especially in our own corner of the world.

Newspapers prosper despite the advent of radio and television, and this book of pictures with stories and memories celebrates 125 years of a regional newspaper, the Manchester Evening News and the community it serves. It has grown as Greater Manchester has grown and we reflect with pride on some of the region's successes and many strengths.

We take you behind the scenes as we look at some of the major news stories and scoops of recent years and give you a brief glimpse of the newspaper operation.

Photographs were chosen from the News archives to record places, events, and achievements, but some, such as this one, were included because we just liked them . . . and a picture can indeed say a thousand words.

We hope you enjoy this nostalgic journey.

Edition time at the old Cross Street offices of the Manchester Evening News and the fleet of Welsh ponies, harnessed to rubber-tyred high-wheeled carts, wait to carry bundles of the Evening News to railway stations and waiting delivery men. These ponies, none more than 15 hands high, were the special joy of early proprietor Mr Russell Allen and were cared for like racehorses at the model stables in Broughton Lane, Salford. Their numbers gradually dwindled owing to the advent of motor-vans, but they were a major form of transporting the newspapers up to March 1952.

The Manchester Evening News.

No. 1. SATURDAY, OCTOBER 10, 1868. ONE HALFPENNY.

TO THE ELECTORS OF THE CITY OF MANCHESTER.—Gentlemen,—I again respectfully present myself to you as a Candidate for the Representation of my native city in Parliament.

That in so short a time as three weeks nearly 11,000 Electors should have signed a Requisition, pledging themselves to do all in their power to secure my return, is a circumstance unprecedented in the history of our elections, and affords a striking proof of the reality of political convictions in Manchester.

Without attaching a personal significance to this manifestation of your opinion, an explanation is easy:—The contest of last winter has impressed you with the belief that in me you have a sound and honest Liberal, not afraid to express his own political views, whilst he respects the rights and feelings of others; and you probably also think that my commercial connection with the prosperity of this city affords a guarantee for my attention to your local wants and interests.

If I mistake not, the country is determined that the State Church in Ireland—the last badge of conquest and ascendancy—shall cease to exist in that country as an Establishment, and assume the position she has so long occupied in Scotland, and now occupies in the Colonies. If we had forced our religious convictions upon the inhabitants of India, or if the inhabitants of Scotland had not freed themselves from the Episcopal Church so alien to their religious instincts, both India and Scotland would at this moment have been as discontented with English rule as Ireland herself.

I am an attached member of the Church of England, and in favour of the union of Church and State in this country—where that union is real, and based upon the willing assent of the nation; but in my humble opinion to talk of the English and Irish Church standing and falling together, is to echo a false cry, highly dangerous to both.

Mr. Gladstone proposes to secure to Ireland the fabric of her cathedrals and churches, her glebe houses, and all private endowments, as well as carefully to respect all existing rights, and to deal only with the future. In the interests of peaceful government I earnestly hope that these terms will be accepted, and that we shall hear no more of levelling up, nor of universal religious endowment.

Education, both in its higher departments in our universities and in its primary forms in our elementary schools, must become truly national and efficient, with equal rights and privileges for all; but I am not prepared to sanction a system of compulsory education, enforced by the policeman or inspector, until it has been shown that the institution of local boards and local machinery have failed in their objects. Place education within reach of the masses, which has never yet been done, and the boon will be accepted for its own sake.

A real and business-like economy has to be enforced upon the Government, not only by a direct reduction of taxation, but also by a thorough departmental reform, especially in our huge military and naval establishments, so that every pound of expenditure shall represent twenty shillings of efficiency.

The vexatious, and in its practical effect, the cruel restrictions on the exercise of the franchise embodied in the rate-paying clauses of the Reform Bill, must be expunged from the Statute book. A vote once granted should be free, and not attended by penalties based on a sham principle. The idea of a *personal* payment of rates was dropped as untenable, and its operation survives only in a shape which, together with an abolition of rate compounding, is productive of the greatest inconvenience and heart-burning amongst the labouring classes.

I am not opposed to Working Men's Associations. Capital expressed by labour, and capital in money have co-equal rights, and their interests are mutual. Preferential protection of either would be unjust. But I have never been able to understand why the funds of Trades' Unions established and employed for legal purposes should be placed beyond the pale of the law, and be subjected to the depredations of dishonest officials. No question of our time more imperatively demands that both sides should be heard than that connected with the labour market and the capital which is to employ that labour; and if I have the honour to become one of the Representatives of this great industrial community, my earnest endeavours will be given towards the solution of these problems.

I have never liked the principle of secret voting, especially when the restricted franchise heretofore in operation made every voter, as it were, the trustee and representative of many of his neighbours. Now that a vote is placed within the reach of the great body of the people, this objection has become correspondingly weakened, and the mechanical conveniences of the ballot, which are indisputable, may with propriety be considered in future legislation. The true remedy for intimidation, however, is to be found in the comparative equalisation of constituencies, and it seems to me a great reflection on our legislation, and on public opinion itself, if we cannot protect a man in the exercise of his vote whilst he records it in the light of day.

Sanitary reform, and the prevention of avoidable sources of mortality—fortunately for the happiness of mankind—greatly occupy public attention, and have naturally engaged much of my time in the earlier part of my life, and I hope the knowledge thus gained may be useful.

Such, gentlemen, are my political principles, which, being honestly entertained, will be honestly advocated. It is impossible, and if possible, it would be undesirable, that all minor differences should be merged in a stagnant uniformity of opinion. Out of discussion and conflict come truth and advancement, and I am sure the Electors of Manchester will pardon the length at which I have endeavoured to lay before them the grounds of my political faith, desiring as I do, above all things, that there shall be no concealment as to my views.—I am, gentlemen, your faithful and obedient servant,

MITCHELL HENRY.

Portland-street, August 11th, 1868.

REPRESENTATION OF MANCHESTER. CANDIDATURE OF MR. MITCHELL HENRY. ELECTION, 1868.—The Committee for conducting the Election of Mr. Mitchell Henry do hereby give notice to all whom it may concern that they will not be responsible for any expenditure incurred without their consent, nor unless an order signed by the secretary or the election agent of Mr. Henry can be produced as a voucher. That they will not pay for the printing of any placards, circulars, or other documents, nor for the insertion of any advertisements which have not been issued by their authority and do not bear official signatures.

The Committee call the special attention of all electors, ward committees, canvassers, and others interested in the election, to the following provisions of the "Corrupt Practices Prevention Act, 1854":—

"17 and 18 Victoria, cap. 102, sec. 4.—Every candidate at an election who shall corruptly by himself or by or with any person, or by any other ways or means on his behalf, at any time either before, during, or after any election, directly or indirectly, give or provide or cause to be given or provided, or shall be accessory to the giving or providing, or shall pay wholly or in part any expenses incurred for any meat, drink, entertainment, or provision to or for any person in order to be elected or for being elected, or for the purpose of corruptly influencing such person or any other person to give or refrain from giving his vote at such election, or on account of such person having voted or refrained from voting or being about to vote or refrain from voting at such election, shall be deemed guilty of the offence of treating, and shall forfeit the sum of £50 to any person who shall sue for the same, with full costs of suit, and every voter who shall corruptly take or accept any such meat, drink, entertainment, or provision, shall be incapable of voting at such election, and his vote, if given, shall be utterly void and of none effect."

And we hereby give notice to all whom it may concern, that the Committee will not be responsible for any payment or other matters forbidden by the above enactments, or any of them, or anywise made or done in contravention of the same.

H. B. JACKSON, Chairman.
CHAS. DURHAM, } Deputy-Chairmen.
C. P. HENDERSON, }
T. C. DAVIES COLLEY, Election Agent.
JAS. NIELD, Hon. Sec.

Central Committee Rooms, 82, Market-street, 2nd October, 1868.

REPRESENTATION OF MANCHESTER. Mr. MITCHELL HENRY'S COMMITTEE SIT DAILY at 82, Market street. Gentlemen desirous of joining the Committee are respectfully requested to forward their names to the Honorary Secretary.

H. B. JACKSON, Chairman.
CHARLES DURHAM, } Vice-Chairmen.
C. P. HENDERSON, }
J. NIELD, Honorary Secretary.

PROFESSOR FAWCETT, M.P., ON CAPITAL AND LABOUR.

On the subject of trade disputes he said:—"Perhaps of the countless topics comprised by the wide subject upon which I am addressing you, it will be well if I ask you to consider whether any new economic arrangements could be adopted which would cause the wealth of this country to give more general happiness and comfort to the whole nation. The most remarkable characteristic of the mode in which industry is carried on amongst us, is the circumstance that capital is supplied by one class, and that labour is supplied by another class; although capital and labour must combine to produce wealth, yet between those who supply the capital and those who supply the labour there often exists no other relations than those between the buyer and the seller of a commodity. The capitalist, or the employer, on the one hand, and the labourer on the other, struggle keenly to obtain as large a share as possible of the aggregate wealth which results from their combined efforts. This struggle often creates unfriendliness, sometimes strife, and occasionally no settlement can be arrived at, no terms are accepted, war is declared, and every one who has had any experience of a strike knows with what fierceness and determination and at what cost this war is often carried on. We are sometimes prone to forget that there is no reason in the nature of things why there should be this economic separation of classes. In England the land is owned by one class, and the capital which is necessary for its cultivation is owned by another class, and the requisite labour is supplied by a body of men whose poverty I may here parenthetically say is proverbial. This mode of carrying on agriculture does not generally prevail in other countries, but may be considered as almost peculiar to England. The inventions of Arkwright and others caused the destruction of hand-loom weaving. It was found that manufactures could be more profitably carried on on a large scale. Extensive buildings, fitted with costly machinery, represent the investment of a large amount of capital. Hence has arisen our modern industrial system, the leading characteristic of which is a complete separation between capital and labour. From this separation manifold evils arise; where it is essential that there should be unity of effort there is often an antagonism of interest. The employer strives to buy labour as cheaply as possible, the employed endeavour to sell their labour at the highest price; hence we have what is aptly described as a labour market, and in this market there often happens that which daily occurs in every mart where commodities are bought and sold. A merchant who has corn to sell cannot obtain for it such a price as he thinks is fair. He resorts to what may be virtually termed a strike; he warehouses his corn, and withdraws it from the market. Labourers who think they cannot obtain a fair price for their labour, withdraw it froun the market, and thus resort to a strike. Many who witness the injury which strikes cause think that the Legislature ought to interfere to prevent them. But it would be as useless and as absurd for the House of Commons to try to forbid labourers withdrawing themselves from the labour market, as it would be to prohibit a merchant warehousing his goods, when he cannot obtain for them a price which he deems reasonable." The tenor of those remarks was to show that strikes could not be prevented by Act of Parliament, but that the cause of the strike being a separation of capital and labour, a remedy for them would be for the labourers to be owners of the capital, the interests of capital and labour would be merged and cease to be antagonistic. "Much of that antagonism of interest, which is the fruitful source of strikes, would be avoided if operatives were allowed directly to participate in profits. This participation may be arranged in various ways. Thus, the Messrs. Crossley, of Halifax, transferred their business into a limited company, the capital of which was £1,650,000; shares representing one-fifth of this capital were reserved for their employées. Workmen were thus enabled to participate in profits, and a certain union between capital and labour was created. The plan has proved eminently successful. The Messrs. Briggs, who are colliery proprietors at Methley, near Leeds, have adopted a plan which effects a more complete union between capital and labour." He believed that courts of arbitration would be only a partial remedy for the evil, though they might be productive of much good. "All will be eager for a change when the evils and the perils resulting from the present state of things are adequately recognised. England has now to carry on in some of her most important branches of industry a keen and closely-contested competition with foreign countries. The slightest additional burden cast upon her may cause the balance to turn against her. Let us, therefore, inquire, 'What are the sources from which peril may come?' At the outset of such an investigation I would lay most emphatic stress upon two maxims. Employers should remember that any deterioration in the condition of our labourers may induce the best and most skilled workmen to emigrate, and the employed should remember that any rise in wages obtained by an undue reduction of their employers' profits may ultimately bring serious loss upon themselves. Capital is always withdrawn from an industry when profits are reduced below the ordinary rate, and capital is the fund from which wages are supplied. It, therefore, becomes evident that on the one hand grave disasters may ensue if employers try to enrich themselves by reducing the earnings of their workmen, or on the other hand, if workmen augment their earnings by diminishing the profit of their employers below the ordinary rate. We, therefore, arrive at the eminently satisfactory conclusion, that those agencies will produce the most permanently beneficial influence, which give additional prosperity to capitalists and labourers alike. I have already shown that such an agency will be brought into operation by the establishment of some system of industrial partnerships."

CONVERTING IRON CUTTINGS INTO BLOOMS.—One always hails with pleasure the utilisation of any waste as so much gained; cotton waste, paper fragments, the washings from woollen factories, have been redeemed from the sewer and the rubbish heap to repay the energy of the inventor, and to supply rising wants with cheap and useful materials: railway grease is in great part supplied by products of the working out of the last of these inventions, and now a very simple and efficacious method of utilising the abundant refuse of the machine shop has just been patented by Mr. Edwd. Hammond Bentall. Iron cuttings, borings, or turnings, are placed in cases of sheet-iron, capable of containing about 1 cwt. of the waste iron; the case, when filled, is submitted to the heat of a reverberatory furnace. When brought to a white heat, it is stamped with stampers, or put under severe pressure, which, owing to the highly-heated and partially-softened state of the metal, will convert it into a solid plastic mass or bloom, possessing a fair grain, and which is capable of being employed for a variety of purposes.

RELICS OF SIR JOHN FRANKLIN'S EXPEDITION.

The *New York Herald* gives the following details of the result, as far as known, of Captain Hall's expedition in search of Sir John Franklin:—

Dr. Goold arrived at New London, Connecticut, a few days since, on board a whaling ship, from Cumberland Inlet, and states that in August, 1867, he spent some considerable time with Mr. Hall, who was then at Repulse Bay. Mr. Hall has traced the fate directly of two of the last survivors of Sir John Franklin's party, and has obtained valuable information regarding the relics and some records reported by the natives to have been left by the lost expedition in King William's Land. Captain Hall learned from some of the Esquimaux, in 1866, that about two years prior to that time Captain Crozier and one of the Franklin crew had died in the vicinity of Southampton Island, while endeavouring to make their way to that place, in the belief that they would be there able to meet a whaler to convey them back to England, or, in fact, anywhere to escape from their arctic prison. Captain Hall is confident of the identity of Captain Crozier with one of the men so described to have perished, as the natives not only gave Captain Crozier's name, but were in possession of certain articles that belonged to him and to his companion. Mr. Hall obtained from these Esquimaux Captain Crozier's watch, a gold chronometer, made by Arnold and Dent, London, besides some small articles of silver and trinkets belonging to their outfit. These relics Mr. Hall now holds, and have been seen and handled by Dr. Goold. Crozier's companion who died with him, is believed to have been a steward of either the Erebus or Terror, as the natives say he was a server of food, but could not recollect his name. The natives also state that they have among them, near Southampton Island, a piece of gold lace and a piece of gold bullion which belonged to Captain Crozier, and is believed to have formed part of one of his epaulettes. They also stated that a number of others had started with Captain Crozier from a place very far north to reach Southampton Inlet, but had perished one by one on the way. They had been passed from one band of Enewits to the other, and when Captain Crozier had passed through two tribes the natives say all further traces were lost, but Captain Hall himself traced the remainder there. Captain Hall also says: "The opinion most entertained is that the natives killed them. They say themselves there was no difficulty in Captain Crozier getting through, because he was accounted among the natives as a first-rate hunter for that country, and could at all times keep himself in food." The records which Captain Hall hopes to be able to secure are in King William's hand, and considerable difficulty is anticipated in the effort to reach them. According to native information the last six survivors built a cairn or rude vault of stones on the rocks, and deposited within it some documents and such articles as they had no further use for, or would have been an encumbrance on their journey. For some time past King William and his tribe have been hostile towards the native followers of King Albert, who inhabit the region about Repulse Bay, where Mr. Hall was quartered, and would allow no incursions into their country. The place where this cairn is described to be situated is about 450 miles northward from Repulse Bay, and in order to reach it Captain Hall has formed an alliance with Albert and his people, and together with his own escort of Europeans, was preparing an expedition of about 90 persons to march in quest of the records. It was Mr. Hall's intention to start in February or March of this year, and he had already accumulated supplies of provisions and other necessaries for the purpose. His force will consist of five Caucasians besides himself, and the remainder would be composed of Alfred's men. Of the whites accompanying him, two were Irish, one German, one Englishman, and one Swede, all of whom were recruited by him from the crew of the Pioneer, which was wrecked in the summer of 1867, at King's Cape. These men are all armed with revolvers and shot guns, and it was mainly through reliance on the Europeans and their weapons that the Albert men were induced to participate in the incursion. Alone they would be unable to cope with King William's forces, who number about two hundred, and could be assembled in a month. Captain Hall would offer no molestation to King William's people, but, if opposed, would give them battle if necessary, as he was determined to obtain the records of the lost explorers if possible. He would be accompanied also by "Joe" and "Hannah," the two Esquimaux or Enewits who, it will be remembered, were a few years ago educated in this country and exhibited in this city. "Joe" and "Hannah" are man and wife, and now form part of Captain Hall's retinue, household, affording him valuable assistance through their knowledge of the English language in communicating with the various tribes of natives, with whose dialects and peculiarities they are familiar. The entire distance, it was expected, would have to be traversed on sledges drawn by dogs, of which useful motive power Mr. Hall has an abundant stock. It was Mr. Hall's determination, if successful in finding the cairn, and no unforeseen circumstances or obstacles intervened, to press still further forward and if possible reach the open Polar Sea and perhaps return by way of Behring Strait. If impeded he expected to return from his expedition to King William's Land about September of 1868, and take up his quarters for the winter at Repulse Bay. Last year he wintered in this locality, and at the time Dr. Goold saw him was in 66 degrees 28 minutes north latitude, and longitude 81 degrees 5 minutes west.

THE MAN IN THE MOON.—The "man in the moon" has been a nickname for mysterious electioneering agents ever since electioneering was an art. But it had dropped out of use latterly, and was only revived again at the time we speak of. The commissioners who sat in the autumn of 1859 succeeded in pinning this denizen of another planet, and compelling him to appear in human flesh and form. On this occasion he turned out to be a Mr. Whitehead, a tradesman of Bradford; and whether he had or had not been recognised while plying his vocation at Wakefield, it seems really quite impossible to say. He was described by one witness as "a very accomplished man"—a man who never kept his hat on in your company. He was a light-haired, pleasant-looking man, sometimes with a beard, sometimes not; but nobody knew who he was. Scores of electors were bribed by him in the openest manner, and hundreds tempted. In fact, Wakefield appears to have been nearly as bad as Saint Albans. In this instance the bribery was of the most wholesale and unguarded character. The evidence is very amusing. Money there was called sugar; and the reception of it, having your hand scratched. The rival candidates were Leatham, Liberal, and Charlesworth, Conservative. One John Jackson had his hand scratched with thirty pounds' worth of the luscious article; but, as thirty-five had been promised, the only effect was to lose his vote and convert him into an active enemy at the same time. His wife, indeed, propitiated by the artful compliment of a Leathamite, to the effect that "women could do anything," tried to persuade her husband to vote for the Liberals; but the more practical Jackson, finding his sugar short weight, soothed his conscience and gratified his vengeance at the same time by voting for Charlesworth. These miscarriages of injustice were not infrequent. We read of "Peter the Jew," who was employed to bribe George Senior, and who, with the cupidity of his race, stopping two pounds out of the money, lost his party the vote in consequence. We find, likewise, that even the great men of all, he of the moon, was occasionally baffled by the dishonesty or astuteness of his customers. "A lady" sold a ham to him for twenty-five pounds, engaging that her husband, who was a Liberal, should vote Conservative; but this heroic woman, more jealous for her husband's honour than her own, kept both the secret and the money, whereby her husband voted with his conscience, and she had "twelve new dresses."—*Cassell's Magazine.*

BEAUTY AND BRAINS.

That lovely woman fulfils only half her mission when she is unpersonable instead of beautiful, all young men, and all pretty girls secure in the consciousness of their own perfections, will agree. Indeed, it is cruel to hear the way in which heady youth despises ugly girls or fading women, however clever, whose charm lies in their cleverness only, with a counteraction in their plainness. To hear them, one would think that hardness of feature, like poverty, was a crime voluntarily perpetrated, and that contempt was a righteous retribution for the offence. Yet their preference, though so cruelly expressed, is to a certain extent the right thing. When we are young, the beauty of women has a supreme attraction beyond all other possessions or qualities, and there are self-evident reasons why it should be so.

It is only as we grow older that we know the value of brains, and, while still admiring beauty—as, indeed, who does not—admire it as one passing by on the other side; as a grace to look at, but not to hold, unless accompanied by something more lasting. This is in the middle term of a man's life. Old age, perhaps with the unconscious yearning of regret, goes back to the love of youth and beauty for their own sake; extremes meeting here as in almost all other circumstances. The danger is when a young man, obeying the natural impulse of his age and state, marries beauty only, with nothing of more durable wear beneath. The mind sees what it brings, and we love the ideal we create rather than the reality that exists. A pretty face, the unworn nerves of youth, the freshness of hope that has not yet been soured by disappointment or chilled by experience, a neat stroke at croquet, and a merry laugh easily excited, made a girl a goddess to a boy who is what he himself calls in love and his friends call spoony. She may be narrow, selfish, spoiled, unfit to bear the burdens of life, and unable to meet her trials patiently; she may be utterly unpractical and silly.

Many a man has cursed, his whole life long, the youthful infatuation that made him marry. Take the case of a rising politician, whose fair-faced wife is either too stupid to care about his position, or else who imperils it by her folly. If amiable and affectionate, and in her own silly little way ambitious, she does him incalculable mischief by exaggeration, and by saying and doing exactly the things that are most damaging to him; if stupid, she is just so much dead weight that he has to carry with him while swimming up the stream. She is very lovely, certainly, and people crowd her drawing-room to look at her; but a plain-featured, sensible, shrewd woman, with no beauty to speak of, but with tact and cleverness, would have helped him in his career far better than would Venus herself if brainless. And so he finds out, when it is too late, to change M for N in the marriage service.

Men do not care for brains in excess in women. They like a sympathetic intellect which can follow them, and seize their thoughts as quickly as they are uttered, but they do not much care for any clear or special knowledge of facts; and even the most philosophic among them would rather not be set right in a classical quotation, an astronomical calculation, or the exact bearing of a political question by a lovely being in tarlatane whom he was graciously unbending to instruct. Neither do they want anything very strong-minded. To most men, indeed, the feminine strongmindedness that can discuss immoral problems without blushing, and despise religious observances as useful only to weak souls, is a quality as unwomanly as a well-developed biceps or a huge fist would be. It is sympathy, not antagonism; it is companionship, not rivalry, still less supremacy, that they like in women; and some women with brains as well as learning—for the two are not the same thing—understand this, and keep their blue stockings well covered by their petticoats. Others, enthusiasts for the freedom of thought and intellectual rights, show theirs defiantly, and meet with their reward. Men shrink from them. Even clever men, able to meet them on their own ground, do not feel drawn to them, while all but high-class minds are dwarfed and humiliated by their learning and their moral courage. And this is what no man likes to feel in the presence of a woman, and because of her superiority. But the brains most useful to women, and most befitting their work in life, are those which show themselves in common sense, in good judgment, and that kind of patient courage which enables them to bear small crosses and great trials alike with dignity and good temper.

A Madrid correspondent of the *Independance* anticipates an interregnum of five or six months, to be followed by the appointment of a foreign Sovereign. He anticipates that the choice of the nation will devolve on the King of Portugal, possibly on a Belgian Prince, or even on "one of the sons of the Queen of England."

THE MUNICIPAL ELECTION.—There are already signs of a contest in some of the Manchester wards in anticipation of next month's elections, and it is not unlikely that party politics will form a prominent feature in the struggle. It is said that among the retiring councillors there are those who have offended their constituents by attending more to the defence of the Irish Church than to the local interests of the citizens. Be that as it may, two of the retiring representatives who are noted "Constitutionalists," viz., Mr. George Anderton in Collegiate Ward, and Mr. John Townsend in St. Clement's Ward are threatened with serious opposition. The former has an opponent in Mr. Wm. Scott Brown (of the firm of Jewsbury and Brown, chemists, Market-street). Mr. Brown addressed the municipal electors at the Merchants' Hotel, Oldham-street. There was a numerous and respectable assembly, and the chair was occupied by Mr. Josiah Taylor. Mr. Brown, in the course of his speech, said he was in favour of an education scheme based upon local taxation and local management, and unsectarian; he should pay particular attention to the sanitary and health committees, and do all he could to diminish the death rate. In answer to questions, he said he would not vote for the reduction of the Town-clerk's salary by one-half; he would support any motion that might be brought forward for the separation of the poor-rates from the borough-rates.—On the motion of Mr. J. Little, seconded by Mr. T. Peel, a resolution, pledging the meeting to assist in securing Mr. Brown's return, was carried unanimously.

PUNISHMENT FOR ADULTERATION OF FOOD IN LONDON IN THE MIDDLE AGES.—In the "Memorials of London," we find that in 1311, a baker was arrested for selling putrid bread, and in 1316 another baker was sentenced to be drawn on a hurdle through the principal streets of the city for selling "light bread deficient in weight;" and in the same year the punishment of the pillory was inflicted upon a man and a woman for selling bread of "rotten materials," and deficient in weight. In 1319 a certain William Spelyng was adjudged to be put upon the pillory, and two putrid beef carcases to be burnt under him for exposing the said carcases for sale; and in 1320 we find two cases similar to the preceding. In 1348 and 1353 the punishment of the pillory was inflicted for selling carrion,—in one case the meat being burnt under the offender. In 1351, proclamations were issued as to the sale of fish. In 1364, a seller of unsound wine was punised by being made to drink it. In the following year the punishment of the pillory was inflicted upon a poulterer for selling putrid pigeons. In 1372 a woman was punished for selling putrid soles; the fish was ordered to be burnt, and the cause of her punishment proclaimed; and we find another case of punishment by the pillory in 1381 for exposing putrid pigeons for sale. In 1390, twelve barrels of eels were ordered to be taken out of the city, and buried in some place underground, lest the air might become infected through the stench arising therefrom. An important proclamation against the adulteration and mixing of wines was issued by Henry V., in 1419, and the punishment of the pillory was ordered for all who sold false wines. If a few examples similar to the above kind were made at the present day they would be of service to the community.

The birth of the news

IF you were a Liberal candidate in 1868, and experiencing great difficulty in obtaining good reports of your meetings in the existing papers, it might seem a logical move to start your own electioneering news sheet.

And, like many others, the man who was to become the founder of the Manchester Evening News did just this. Mitchell Henry was born in Ardwick in 1833, the son of a well known textile merchant. He was an eminent consulting surgeon, deeply concerned about the state of sanitation and public health in Britain. On the death of his father, he relinquished his medical career to take over the family business and, when all was running smoothly, he turned to politics to try to improve standards.

On October 10, 1868, the first eight-page issue of his electioneering broadsheet was published and given out at a celebration dinner at the Woolsack Hotel. It went on sale for one half-penny at 3 pm each day.

This first issue, and all others up to election day, published Mr Henry's election pledge on the front page and gave reports of his meetings, plus names of his supporters and committee members. The appointed editor, Mr T Broscombe, made a serious attempt at injecting newsworthy items such as reports of the Liverpool and Manchester Stock Markets, readers' letters and even advertisements before election day on Tuesday, November 17. On this day, according to the paper, Henry made a noble act of self sacrifice and, at 1 pm, retired from the contest to prevent a catastrophe to the Liberal cause. Perhaps if he had started the Manchester Evening News a few months earlier, he might have stood a better chance of success. As it was, he decided to sell his broadsheet to John Edward Taylor, son of J E Taylor who was the first proprietor of the Manchester Guardian, and his brother in law Peter Allen.

It is interesting to note that Mr. Henry became a member of Parliament for County Galway three years later and did important work for Irish agriculture.

The leading article in the first issue of the Manchester Evening News began: "In putting ourselves into print we have no apology to offer, but the assurance of an honest aim to serve public interests . . ."

This aim has continued for 125 years and the words are still valid today.

Above we see a nineteenth century scene on a busy Manchester street with a young newspaper seller.

On the left is a reproduction of the first issue of the Manchester Evening News.

Early days . . .

In 1868 the world was on the threshold of a new era and the Liberals were being swept to power after promising to set afoot a vast new range of social reforms.

And in Manchester, central powerhouse of the industrial revolution, was being mirrored the first of those reforms as the exaggerated individualism of the early Victorian years gave way to the collective state.

The death rate in Manchester that year was the highest in Britain — a grim tribute to the development of a typical nineteenth-century industrial city. But Manchester appointed its first Medical Officer of Health, Dr Leigh, who made it his first task to examine the city's unenviable position as one of the most unhealthy towns in the Kingdom.

Something at last was about to be done. And indeed, not all of the city was ailing. Opportunity abounded as the British Empire reached the peak of its power and fortunes were to be made in the north.

A bustle of activity at the top of a relatively prosperous looking Cross Street where horse-drawn trams and carts dominate the scene in this early photograph.

On the left is the Examiner building in Pall Mall, Manchester, later to be demolished to make room for the new Manchester Guardian and Evening News building in 1929.

The poultry market, Shudehill, Manchester.

Another view of Shudehill Market around the turn of the century from a photographer of the day.

Shawls and clogs, good humour and good neighbourliness of the Lancashire mill-girls typifies the spirit of these days.

These two young girls with their white 'pinnies' have just been to the 'jug and bottle' shop for jugs of beer.

A picture from a reader shows a general store in Greengate, Salford.

A scene in Bank Street, Manchester.

Lunch break outside Sacred Trinity Church on Salford's famous 'Flat Iron' market.

Goods are loaded up on to horse-drawn carts outside Smithfield Market, Manchester.

Shire horses pull the carts in this early morning turnout.

On the left is an early drawing of the Manchester Guardian and Evening News Building in Cross Street. The close links with the Manchester Guardian continued and were strengthened in 1924 when John Russell Scott bought the Manchester Evening News. The two papers were brought together under one ownership, while maintaining their individuality and editorial independence. The paper was printed at Cross Street until 1970 when the company moved to premises on Deansgate.

Below - St Ann's Square in the 1890's with a line up of hansom cabs.

The building on the left was the old Manchester Infirmary, in what is now Piccadilly Gardens.

Another view of Manchester with the Cotton Exchange in the distance and the Grosvenor Hotel on the right-hand side of the picture.

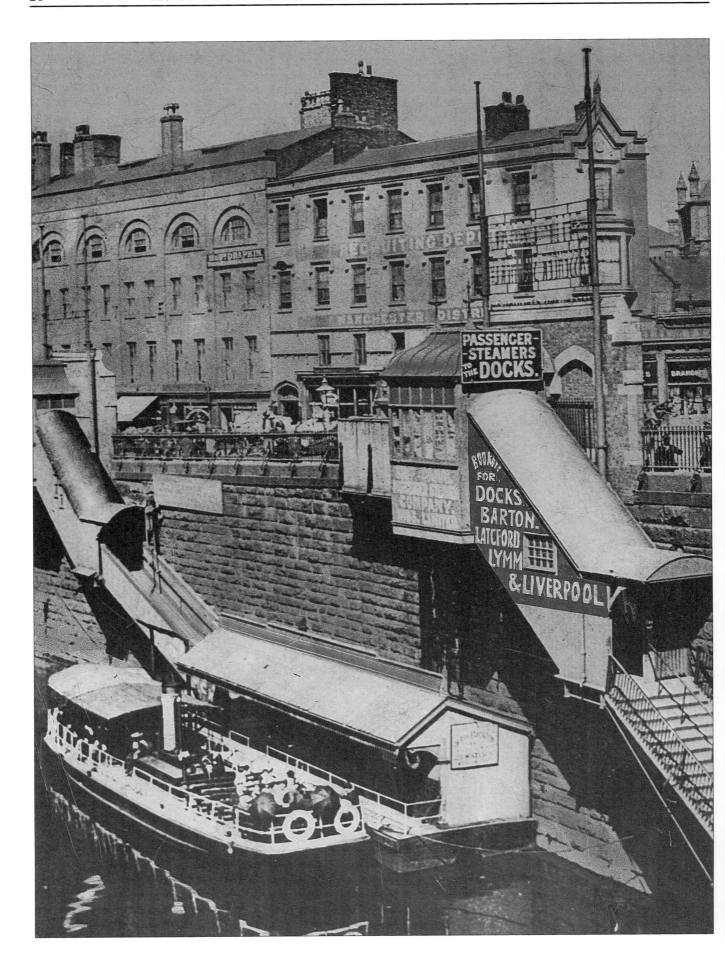

Lure of the waterways

1884, and a steamer takes on passengers on the River Irwell near Manchester Cathedral. Chetham's School is in the background. Sailings to Pomona Gardens were very popular with courting couples, who liked to watch the eel-catchers, admire views of Trafford Park woodlands and gaze at the peaceful farms and orchards. But the increasing smells from the river stopped it all. Fishing in the Irwell ended about 1850 (an 18lb salmon was caught near Warrington in 1840).

The picture on the right shows a boatman resting at the stern of his craft at Hulme Locks on the Bridgewater Canal.

Below is an early view of St Margaret's Bridge, and the River Irwell.

Left: Decked out in May Day Parade finery is one of Paulden's horse-drawn delivery vans. William Paulden, a showman as well as a shrewd businessman, attracted customers to his Stretford Road shop by spectacular window displays, sometimes with live lions and tigers. A draper, he also sold stout furniture and hard wearing lino at cheap prices. The store is now Debenhams.

Below: Wilsons, a grocer's shop in Regent Road, Salford.

They brought the sea to Manchester's doorstep

COURAGE and enterprise built the Manchester Ship Canal.

Towards the end of the 19th century, Manchester was declining fast as a city. One reason was that the railways were charging nearly twice as much as those on the Continent. But even more damaging were the ever-growing charges and dock dues at Liverpool.

For an Oldham spinner it was cheaper to buy cotton in Germany or France, ship it to Hull, and then send it by rail to Oldham, than to buy in Liverpool.

Manchester had to find an answer or die.

It took three years to push and coax the necessary Bill through Parliament and when at last Daniel Adamson, who had set the scheme rolling, came home successful from London, workers took the horses from his carriage and dragged him home, cannons were fired, church bells rang and bands played.

Raising the money was the next struggle. One necessary item even before the work could start was the purchase of the Bridgewater Navigation Company's property and the £1,710,000 cheque for that was the largest ever drawn up to that time.

Enough finance was arranged to justify going on, and on November 11, 1887, Lord Egerton of Tatton, who succeeded Adamson as chairman of the Manchester Ship Canal Company, cut the first sod at Eastham. Then, with work well under way, the weather brought new worries.

Unprecedented storms and floods destroyed overnight the work of months. Again a few months later, more storms left six miles of excavated canal bed 40 feet under water in places. Ice and snow followed.

All this meant extra expense, and to make matters worse, the Bridgewater Canal, the only profit-making asset the directors had, was frozen and out of action. More money was needed, and there was no time to raise it by public appeal. So it came about that Manchester City Council unanimously approved assistance to the extent of £3M. Then in 1892 it was reported that another £1¼M was necessary to finish the work. To be on the safe side, the City Council made £2M available, with the proviso that the Corporation should have a majority on the Board of Directors.

The Manchester Ship Canal celebrates its centenary in 1994.

Navvies digging Manchester Ship Canal: 16,000 of them were employed on the great project.

Placing sandstone pitching on the canal bank.

Barton Bridge under construction.

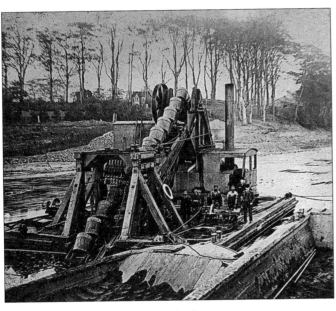

A bucket dredger.

Splitting rock for removal and re-use as pitching on canal banks.

The inside of one of the syphons carrying the River Gowy under the canal at Stanlow, Ellesmere Port.

One of the steel lattice booms of a railway viaduct under construction.

Driving piles to form Coffer dam.

Shropshire Union Canal lighthouse at Ellesmere Port.

Dutch fascine workers labouring on the canal banks.

Steam grab removing excavation.

Original pumping station at Eastham locks.

Inspecting the Weaver sluices.

The first big ships sailed up to Manchester on January 1, 1894, and on May 21, 1894, the official opening was performed by Queen Victoria on board the yacht Enchantress. This painting commemorated the occasion. The total cost of the canal was about £15m. In the first year 925,000 tons of traffic entered the Port of Manchester, 1896 saw that figure doubled.

Manchester received a Royal visit after the opening of the Ship Canal. Streets and buildings along the eight-mile route of the procession were gaily decorated. In the full page we see a triumphal arch of fire escape ladders over Deansgate. Two million people turned out to cheer the Queen on that day.

The Canal brought in the expected new trade. Warehouses and offices mush-roomed around Manchester Docks and Trafford Park. On the right is the entrance to the Park in 1905 when the No 9 dock was opened on the site of the New Barns Racecourse.

The Boer War . . .

1899 The Boer War — The dead and injured lie in the trenches as the soldiers fight on from behind the barricades.

A blindfolded emissary is brought to discuss terms of surrender after the Boer defeat at Paaderberg.

The end of an Era

DEATH OF THE QUEEN.

RECORD OF A NOBLE LIFE.

SPECIAL MEMOIR.

With profound regret we have to announce that the illness of Her Majesty the Queen has terminated fatally.

The death of Queen Victoria was recorded on page three of the newspaper on January 22, 1901. After a reign of over 50 years, when the majority of Britons had known no other monarch, it was the end of an momentous era. The days of the Empire were already fading with the Boer War and conflict in India and the dark days of the First World War were not far ahead.

The Boer War dragged out from 1899 to 1902, and there were many celebrations when it ended like this procession seen in Portland Street. But much livelier jubilation had marked some of the turning-points of the war, and one of them even gave a new word to the language — 'Mafficking'.

Early reporting staff

AS with all great newspapers, the reputation of the Manchester Evening News has been built up on a succession of resourceful, far-sighted editors and on succeeding generations of newsmen — reporters, photographers, sub editors — dedicated to the single-minded task of keeping their newspaper ahead of the news.

After Mr T Broscombe, Hugh Wilson was appointed editor and was paid £3 per week for his services. The reporter — only one in those early days — received 25 shillings.

James Parkinson, a long serving editor held the position for many years and was passionately fond of cricket. He saw little purpose in any other sport and preferred his reporters to be similarly enthusiastic.

He was succeeded by W A Balmforth, who served the paper with distinction for over 25 years. It was under his direction that the 'News' began to take shape as a family newspaper with the aim to keep its columns clean and wholesome, while still reporting important, if sometimes distasteful news.'

Balmforth was followed by Henry Archer who, in the late twenties made the revolutionary decision to put news instead of adverts on the front page.

Then came W J Haley who re-shaped the paper and it was under his editorship that the Manchester Evening News made enormous strides. By 1939 it had become the biggest evening paper outside London and still maintains this position in 1993.

Three pm and the 'pony expresses' tear out of Cross Street and into Market Street to the delight of bystanders.

FROM THE
"MANCHESTER EVENING NEWS" REPORTING STAFF, 1903-4.
TO THEIR CHIEF, MR W. A. BALMFORTH, XMAS, 1904.

This unusual group picture, which shows all the members of an early reporting staff of the Manchester Evening News in 1903 with their Editor William Balmforth, was presented on March 5, 1904 at the Dorchester Hotel, London where the jubilee dinner of the National Union of Journalists was held. The Union was founded in Manchester in 1906, and the actual founder, W N Watts (No 9), became its first general secretary. This picture is unique because, not only are several of the original or early officials of the Union shown, but every member of staff was at some time in one or other of Press causes, the National Union of Journalists, the Institute of Journalists, the Newspaper Press Fund, or the Manchester Press Club.

The professional photographer at work: The large camera on sturdy tripod, an equally sturdy packing case for the operator to stand on. The occasion was the inauguration of Manchester's first electrified tram route on June 6, 1901. The line of new electric trams, bedecked with flowers and potted palms and filled with top-hatted and bewhiskered City Fathers made its way from Albert Square to Cheetham Hill, where the Lord Mayor officially opened the Queen's Road Depot.

A red-letter day at Walkden — the first tramcar arrives, on June 22, 1906. The crowd is 'working class', but note that even the schoolboys are wearing stiff collars.

Trams

FROM 1865 Manchester had enjoyed a flourishing public transport service run with the unified control of the Manchester Carriage Company. By 1870 there were three-horse omnibuses providing services along most of the city's main roads. But they were still the transport of the well-to-do. After the introduction of carriages drawn by horses in 1877 in both Manchester and Salford, the tramcar became an institution. In 1901 the first motorised tramcar made its appearance and within two years, in a massive undertaking, almost the whole of the system had been converted to electric traction. It became an affordable means of transport for all.

Standing room only! One of the first trams arrives at Albert Square, Manchester, to pick up passengers.

It is 3 30 pm on June 12, 1906, as crowds line the street at Sale Moor village to greet 496, the special car which opened the new route.

King Edward VII and Queen Alexandra arrive on July 13, 1905, for the unveiling of the Lancashire Fusiliers monument in Oldfield Road, Salford.

When General Booth founded his Salvation Army in 1878, he and his followers were regarded as a nuisance and trouble makers. By 1902 the value of his work was officially recognised when King Edward VII invited him to be present at his Coronation. In 1910 the General made an almost royal progress through Eccles as this News picture of the time shows.

Here are the residents of Silk Street, Salford, posing for the camera at the street party held in honour of the coronation of King George V on June 22, 1911.

Belle Vue was a popular entertainment centre opened in 1835 by another visionary, Arthur Jennison. It held many attractions, including a zoo, and was set amid beautiful gardens. The picture shows the Chinese tearoom.

Manchester turns out to greet their Royal Highnesses King George V and Queen Mary on their State visit to the city on July 14, 1913.

On the same day, spectators in Peel Park, Salford, await the arrival of the King and Queen who will perform the official opening of the Technical Institute. The King had acceded to the throne only three years before.

An unusually posed group of members of the Manchester Fire Brigade at their headquarters in Jackson's Row in 1898.

These were times of unrest and here we see a detachment of police from Oldham having just arrived at Victoria Station for strike duty in Manchester in August, 1911.

Advertising has played an enormous part in the success of the Manchester Evening News. From as early as the sixth issue in 1868, advertisements started to appear. In November of the same year a notice giving a 'classification of advertisements' was published. For 'tuppence' per line - paid prior to insertion, readers could advertise for Situations - Apartments, vacant or wanted - Money to be 'lent' or wanted - Partnerships - Houses - and Sales by Private Contract. These adverts were a great selling point for the paper and appeared on the front page. The leader column and news appeared on page three. Even important news items such as the death of Queen Victoria, as we saw earlier, was consigned to the inner pages.

Votes for women

Famous suffragette Mrs Emmeline Pankhurst made her entry into political life as the bride of Dr Pankhurst who was one of the founders of the Women's Suffrage Society.

As his wife she gained confidence by helping him in his work and after his death, with her daughters Christabel and Sylvia plus a few women friends formed the Women's social and political union.

She was arrested twelve times and jailed on several occasions. She died at the age of 70 in 1928 after having lived just long enough to see the passing of the Act which gave full and equal suffrage to men and women in.

Her house in Plymouth Grove, Manchester, is now a museum.

Mrs Emmeline Pankhurst being removed by the law during a demonstration at Buckingham Palace gates.

Mrs Pankhurst is on the right with Mrs Baines of Stockport who shared imprisonment with her.

On the left, standing with Christabel Pankhurst, is Mary Cawthorp a Yorkshire organiser, who started the protest in the House of Commons. On the extreme right in the trap is Adela Pankhurst, daughter of Christabel.

When Henry Ford decided to expand into the English car market with his highly popular and affordable Model T, he chose Manchester as his base, opening his factory and shop in Trafford Park in 1911.

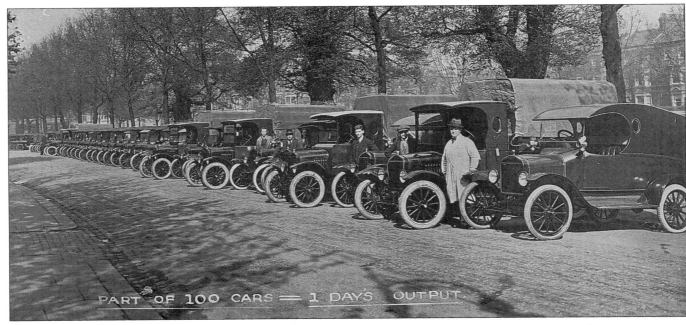

All gleaming and new these Ford cars and vans are lined up outside the factory in Trafford Park. In just one day 100 cars were produced.

Rolls and Royce

The world renowned Rolls-Royce. Henry Royce built his first 10hp 2-cylinder Royce motor car at his factory in Cooke Street, Manchester in 1904. A year later he met investor the Hon Charles Stuart Rolls in the Midland Hotel and the Rolls-Royce company was formed. The 40hp Silver Ghost was soon designed and made the firm world famous. His engines also powered early aircraft and are still regarded as the most reliable engines in the world.

Frederick Henry Royce.

The Hon Charles Stewart Rolls.

Was this a rally of Rolls-Royce cars? Whatever the occasion, it brought four models together at the summit of the Buxton-Macclesfield Road, outside the Cat and Fiddle Inn.

The high flyers of AVRO

Brothers Alliot Vernon Roe (left) and Humphrey V Roe in earlier days with their wood and canvas aircraft.

An Avro Type E being transported through Manchester in 1910.

The new Avro Aldershot giant bomber 850 photographed at Alexandra Park where, along with another similar machines after final tests, have been taken over by the RAF. These machines were all metal.

Alliot Vernon Roe, the pioneer flyer and aeroplane builder was born in 1877 in Patricroft.

An engineer and designer, his spare time interest was building model aircraft, which he entered for competitions. He also corresponded with the Wright Brothers in America on the subject of gliding.

One of his brothers, Humphrey was a partner in a surgical webbing company in Brownsfield Mill, Great Ancoats Street and offered finance for a full scale powered aeroplane named The Bullseye after a brand of gents braces manufactured by Horace. On July 13, 1909 with Alliot at the controls, it made a flight of 100ft, which is accepted by many authorities as the first recorded flight by a British flyer in a British built machine.

The first planes were constructed at the Mill by the newly formed AVRO company and advertising at the time stated that 'AVRO planes are held up by Bullseye braces'.

For the War, the factory supplied Gnome engined biplanes to the Central Flying School and in 1913 production was transferred to a site in Clifton Street, Miles Platting, where the famous AVRO 504 biplane became the standard product. It was designed by Roy Chadwick, architect of the World War II Lancaster Bomber.

An historic take-off . . . the Lancashire Aero Club first aircraft making its debut flight in 1922 from Alexandra Park, Manchester. At the controls of the home-made glider is founder member, Mr John Leeming.

Gallant Colonel Cody and his biplane photographed in Blackpool in 1910 by Walter Doughty a celebrated 'News' photographer. The plane, a flimsy thing of bamboo and canvas is being swept away by a gust of wind while Cody and his helpers desperately try to hold it. A moment later it overturned completely and was a crumpled wreck. Such were the trials and tribulations of these early aviators.

Your Country Needs You

IT was a perfect summer that year of 1914, which was only as it should be, for it was to mark the end of an era and set the world on a trail of war and disaster on a scale never imagined.

The first lightning flash came late in June, when an Austrian Archduke was killed by an assassin's bullet. That was the spark that set alight the powder kegs of World War One.

This was to be the war to end all wars, and our armies were to return to a land fit for heroes to live in. Alas, it was no such thing, and the years following the war were years of poverty, of depression, of unemployment and hunger.

A recruiting officer finds a not too willing listener during a recruiting campaign in Manchester during the First World War.

A blanket tossing interlude for the Manchester Volunteer Battalions in training at Heaton Park in 1914/15. A typical day began at 6 am, an hour of drill from 6 30 to 7 30 followed by breakfast and then training parades. The day ended at 11 15 with lights out.

On March 21, 1915 — Exactly three years to the day before the Battle of Manchester Hill was fought — the 16th Manchester's marched past Lord Kitchener at Manchester Town Hall with the rest of the City Battalions.

Below, 1919 — Coming home: Men of the 8th Battalion The Manchester Regiment marching along London Road, Manchester, on their return from Belgium. Captain Stewart is leading.

Broughton House, Salford was created in 1916 as a home for ex-servicemen and still exists today. The money for the home was raised by Colonel Sir William Coates who also formed a company of stretcher bearers for the Boer War and later helped form the Territorial Army.

Following World War I, Captain John William Alcock, DSC (left), and Lieutenant Arthur Whitton-Brown put their dreams to practical test, and made them come true by making the first non-stop Transatlantic flight, 1,950 miles in 15 hours and 57 minutes from Newfoundland to Ireland.

King George and Queen Mary, with Princess Mary, during their visit on October 8, 1921, to open the reconstructed Royal Exchange. On the left of the Lord Mayor, Alderman W (later Sir William) Kay is the Recorder, Mr A H Ashton, KC. To the right of the Lady Mayoress is the Town Clerk, Mr T Hudson. Lord Derby is behind Queen Mary, and on the left is Chief Constable, Sir Robert Peacock.

Rutherford and Geiger (left) counting alpha-rays in Manchester. Ernest Rutherford was a professor of physics at Manchester University who, in 1918, headed the team which first split the atom. One of his valuable collaborators at the university was Hans Geiger, the inventor of the first version of the particle counter, who joined the staff from Germany.

Manchester Whit Walks which took place during Wakes Week were the highlight of the year. The children, dressed in their 'Sunday best' paraded through the streets. Our picture shows an Italian Society group, carrying a statue of the Madonna and Child.

Back-to-back neighbourliness and dancing to a barrel organ in the street.

A popular outing in 1928 was a trip aboard the Royal Daffodil along the Ship Canal to New Brighton. Here we see excited children going aboard.

'Sunday best' was the rig of the day for everyone aboard this heavily laden barge on a Whitsun Thursday outing along the
Bridgewater Canal.

Another popular pastime was cycling, and here we see a club passing through Alderley Edge.

Hard Times

Heartbreaking though unemployment can be, it was even grimmer in the 1930's when the dole was pitifully small and to be out of work meant that families went hungry. Full scale protest marches were organised in the main cities including Manchester. These pictures show some of the scenes at this sad time.

This street on the right is typical of the living conditions in the early thirties. It was listed for demolition under a slum clearance scheme.

Below on the right gives a view of a traffic jam in Manchester. A patient horse in the foreground is pulling a load of 'Quinine Champagne' and a lorry loaded with cotton waste follows a Manchester Evening News van to head up Market Street.

With miners on strike in 1926, women with scarves round their heads, and a man search a spoil heap near Manchester for fuel.

An inevitable part of the industrial scene, the strike pickets. These at Burnley in October 1931 look more weary than militant, but the women raise a smile for the press photographers.

The mounted police had to control the crowds of men waiting hopefully near Aytoun Street 'labour exchange'.

There were many ugly incidents. Here the Manchester Fire Brigade returns from a riot incident in Market Street.

On the right we see an orderly protest march against unemployment, at the junction of Portland Street and Oxford Street, Manchester.

When 30 jobs were advertised for Queen's Park Hippodrome, Harpurhey, a queue of over 1,000 people had formed before midday.

On the morning of September 26, 1931, Mahatma Gandhi, the Hindu politician and leader of the National Congress party in India, called on these people in Darwen. For his visit he was the guest of Charles Haworth of Darwen. Gandhi publicly proclaimed that the poverty he saw in Lancashire disturbed him but it was not, he said, anything like so terrible as that of his people in India. Gandhi was assassinated by a Hindu fanatic in 1948.

A queue for a tram in the thirties.

To queue . . . or not to queue?

Passengers for tramcars and buses must form a queue' said a new regulation made in 1933. The law was not always obeyed as our photographer records in Albert Square the same day.

A 1931 view of the Manchester Central Library beginning to take shape in St Peter's Square. The Waldorf Restaurant and St Peter's Hotel originally stood on this site.

King George V and Queen Mary at the entrance of the City's new Central Library in 1934, as they perform the official opening ceremony.

An advertisement from the paper promotes the film The Love Parade starring Maurice Chevalier and Jeanette MacDonald at the Paramount Theatre.

One of the Manchester city centre cinemas which never really made it. The Piccadilly, next to the State Cafe was a popular teatime rendezvous in the Thirties.

Musical impresario, C B Cochrane (left) outside the Midland Hotel talking to composer, Cole Porter.

Here is C B Cochrane with some of his principals arriving for rehearsals of his review 'Streamline' which opened at the Opera House. With 'C B' are (left to right) Miss Florence Desmond, Miss Nora Howard and Madamoiselle Meg Leconnier.

At a gathering at the Paramount Theatre in October 1937, we see (from the left) Herbert Wilcox, Sybil Thorndike, Anna Neagle and Marie Burke.

Singer and film star Gracie Fields with the Mayor of Rochdale during her visit in 1931.

Jessie Matthews and her husband Sonnie Hale meet some of the girls dressed for a tableaux in costumes of all nations before performing the opening ceremony at the gala launching of the Gaumont.

Amy, Wonderful Amy . . . Britain's queen of the air, Amy Johnson who became Mrs Jim Mollison arriving at Barton Aerodrome on a visit to Manchester on October 31, 1931.

Salford historical pageant, and another excuse for a street party.

Manchester University Rowing Club's boat looks far too big a load for this small car which took it from Manchester over the Pennines for York Regatta.

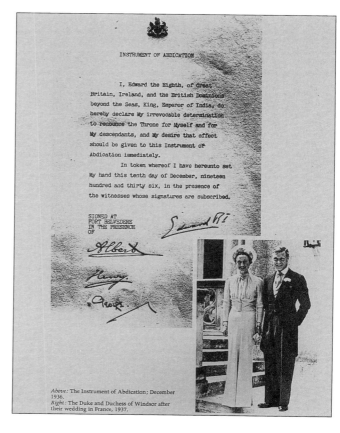

Above: The Instrument of Abdication; December 1936.
Right: The Duke and Duchess of Windsor after their wedding in France, 1937.

On December 10, 1936 after the shortest reign in British history, Edward VIII shocked the nation by renouncing the Throne for himself and his descendents. He wished to marry divorcee Mrs Wallis Simpson which was not acceptable for a King of England. On 3 June, 1937, one year after his abdication they were married in France at the Chateau de Caude where they were photographed by Cecil Beaton.

These ladies of Walter Street, Harpurhey get ready for the Coronation of George VI, the shy brother of the popular Edward VIII who had abdicated the previous year. The flags are hung across the street, the roads are swept and the pavements are scrubbed clean ready for the festivities

In Manson Street, Ardwick Green, this street party is in full swing as the children wave for the camera.

On the right one of Manchester's most distinguished shopping streets is impressively decked out in white and gold banners for the Coronation of King George VI.

Early memories

Bob Corfield — From copy boy in 1934 to proof reader and then staff photographer. He retired in 1984. Here are some of his pre-war memories.

My first encounter with the MEN was way back in 1934 when I was thrown in at the deep end into the hurly burly of newspaper production at the age of fourteen. I started as a copy boy - which was the bottom rung of the ladder in newspapers.

The Managing Editor then was William Haley, a large man in more than just physical size and we called him 'Big Bill'. He was a work-aholic and expected his staff to be likewise, but from the copy boys upwards he was well respected and admired.

Many a time I have known him to work all through the night. He had an old camp bed in his office to catch up on a couple of hours sleep when he worked late on a story. But behind all his bluff exterior he was a caring man and knew how to handle his staff and get the best out of them. I can recall him sending me personal Air Mail letters during the war while I was serving with the RAF in India. And this, for a very busy and important man, was a wonderful thing to do as they were hand written, not typed out notes from his secretary.

He was later knighted and went on to become Editor of the Times and Director General of the BBC.

The actual Editor at this time was a Mr H W Archer, a quiet, unassuming man, the exact opposite of Bill Haley. He wrote a humorous column each week under the pen name of Percy Phlage as well as his brilliant leader columns.

After spending 18 months as a copy boy I was given a more permanent job, that of copy-holder to a proof reader in the Readers' department, where all the copy was checked and corrected before going to press. A boring job to me but a completely different atmosphere from the chaos of the sub-editor's room at 3, Cross Street.

News Editors I can remember from the late 1930's up to the outbreak of war were Ted Castle, who later was married to MP Barbara Castle, John Beavan later to become Lord Ardwick - and of course Frank Allaun, a great Labour man who left to work on the Daily Herald and then became MP for Salford.

The war then interrupted my career at the MEN for six years.

Bob Corfield's photograph of the Editor William Haley (in the centre) making a presentation to Rupert Denny surrounded by his staff. On the very right of the picture, seen over someone's shoulder is Evening News journalist Tom Jackson, who was killed in the Manchester United air crash.

The R100, created by Sir Dennis Burney who worked for Crossley Motors, is seen above the rooftops of Manchester in the early thirties. Although it was not used during the war this picture seems to epitomise the feeling of impending disaster.

All the top lawns and flower-beds surrounding the sunken gardens in Piccadilly, Manchester, were dug up when work began to build surface brick and concrete air-raid shelters.

Preparing for war

DESPITE only two decades having passed since the 'war to end all wars', on September 3, 1939, Britain was again at war.

The Manchester Evening News played an important role in guiding, calming and influencing the people of Manchester. Not only was it the main means of reporting the local war effort, it was sometimes the only link with home for those serving overseas.

The News had given extensive coverage to the run up to the war. In 1933 the paper greeted the succession of Hitler as German Chancellor with horror, pointing out the implications of his rise to power. The credit for giving the News this serious political outlook went to editor William Haley who had consistently opposed Prime Minister Chamberlain's foreign policy. In his editorial of August 25 he asked readers "can any life be worth living in which force and not justice governs the affairs of nations and men".

So Manchester prepared for war.

Manchester men of the 8th Manchester Regiment (Ardwick) marching to the station for duty in France — 1939.

An Anderson shelter in Chorlton-cum-Hardy.

Cut out of solid rock, in the caves below Chestergate, Stockport, this ARP shelter was intended to provide accommodation for 4,000 people. It was part of a £22,000 scheme to provide bomb-proof shelter for 20,000 people. It is now a museum.

The completed surface air raid shelters in Piccadilly Gardens

Gas masks and the great evacuation

On September 1, 1939 the evacuation of Manchester's schoolchildren got under way. The Manchester Evening News attempted to convince the public of the wisdom of the measure, and of the efficiency of the process. But it was a poignant day.

The bombs did not fall on Manchester and its surrounding towns and cities immediately - but fall they did. Perhaps it was a sensible move after all to send our children to the comparative safety of the country.

Children being introduced to the wearing of gas masks at St Joseph's police premises, Longsight — September, 1938.

WHAT TO TAKE

THESE are what evacuees should have when reporting for transfer to the safe areas :

SCHOOL CHILDREN

Gas mask, change of underclothing, night clothes, house shoes, spare stockings, toothbrush and comb, towel and handkerchiefs, warm coat or macintosh, and a packet of food sufficient for 24 hours.

BABIES

Dried milk for two days, 2 vests, 1 pilch, 6 napkins, 1 matinee coat, 1 pair leggings, 2 nightdresses, 1 woollen body belt, rainproof for cot, 1 pair socks, 1 shawl, safety pins, soap, towel, sponge, feeder, feeding bottle, gas mask.

TODDLERS

2 vests, 2 pairs of rompers, 3 pairs of knickers, 2 pairs of socks, shoes, or gym shoes, 2 nightdresses, and a gas mask.

MOTHERS

1 gas mask, change of clothing, 1 toothbrush, hairbrush, comb, small-tooth comb, handkerchiefs, 1 stamped addressed postcard, 1 pencil, needle, cotton, mending wool, fork, spoon, mug, plate, electric torch, and fruit and sandwiches for one day.

Parents anxiously wait to see their children board the buses taking them to comparative safety outside the city centres

It's a serious business being labelled like a parcel and packed off across the country away from your family.

Boys from Burnage High School, Manchester, calmly board a bus to take them to the station.

Britain's first Airborne Forces trained in large numbers at Manchester's airport during the Second World War.

Ringway control tower during the war years. The aeroplane is an Avro Lincoln.

Ft-Lt F G Fray briefing pilots of No 613 (City of Manchester) Squadron, Royal Auxiliary Air Force, before they left Ringway Airport for training exercises.

Vampire aircraft of no 613 (City of Manchester) Squadron of the Royal Auxiliary Air Force were a familiar sight at Manchester Airport in the early years.

Army personel and firefighters crowd round this mobile canteen which was the gift to Great Britain from the people of Trinidad and Tobago — Manchester, 1940.

A grim reminder of the consequences of war. A mobile blood transfusion unit in Piccadilly with volunteer blood donors.

Designed by Roy Chadwick of AVRO, the Lancaster Bomber was the best bomber produced by any nation in World War II. They flew from Ringway in 1941 and were made at Woodford, Chadderton, Trafford Park, Ringway, Chester and Canada.

Decontamination squads at work at Altrincham Gas Precautions School, now the headquarters of British Gas.

Manchester Evening News

Bombs Shower on City: Shelterers Trapped in Wreckage

MANCHESTER BLITZ : MANY BUILDINGS FIRED

TWO RAIDERS BELIEVED DOWN IN NORTH-WEST: VIVID FLASH—SILENCE

MANCHESTER had its longest and most severe aerial bombardment last night. For many hours hundreds of incendiary and explosive bombs were dropped, and a pall of smoke hung over the city to-day.

The raid started shortly after dusk, when enemy raiders, apparently approaching the city from the south, spread fanwise over a wide area and adopted the familiar tactics of flare dropping, followed by incendiary bombs at various points.

Wave after wave of planes roared over the city every few minutes, and targets for the later arrivals were made with the fires started.

The whole resources of the city's fire brigade services, including auxiliary firemen, were at their posts ready to deal with the outbreak. Some of the fires cast a deep red glow in the sky, which was visible for miles.

Later high explosives and incendiaries dealt death to people and destruction to property.

Hospitals, shops, hotels, and business premises were damaged.

The number of casualties has not yet been estimated. Most of the fires had been got under control, thanks to the magnificent work of the firemen who worked, hereically hour after hour, regardless of the serious risk they ran in carrying on while the raiders droned overhead.

Hospital Hit

When the raid started many people were caught in the streets, and suffered from the effects of damage from the air raids. A number of shops had windows shattered, and several were damaged by fire.

There were reports too of people being trapped when buildings were damaged in various parts of the city, and rescue squads were still working to free them 17 hours after the raid started.

Flash in Sky

Two raiders are believed to have been brought down.

★ **Turn to Back Page**

Chins Up in the North-West

MANCHESTER, bombed for hours during the night, is chin up to-day. Manchester, like London, Coventry, and the rest, can take it.

The staffs of Manchester's shops, offices, and warehouses went to work to-day, not as usual, but with determination that their duty to the war and the spirit should be business as usual.

many premises they went on, making light of bombs and improvising and necessary repairs had been carried out.

Their attitude to the Blitz was on a par with that shown in many incidents of that raid.

...es who remained on duty at a Manchester hospital to comfort patients had a fitting reward. They saved their own lives. They, however admiring the hospital received a direct hit.

Two maids were killed. Some people are still believed buried beneath the wreckage. The patients, move or where, were injured, have been evacuated. A helper said "All the nurses' thoughts have been for their patients."

An A.F.S. man named Warburton climbed into the blazing front bedroom of a house and rescued an old woman and her two daughters. The woman sustained slight burns.

One shop, selling jewels, pearls, and perfumes was intact except for a small bottle of perfume which had been shattered. It was called "SIN."

Workers from a Manchester branch office of the National A.R.P. for Animals Association collected scores of cats and dogs which had been bombed out.

Mr. Joseph Bradley, a baker, who was going to his work in the early evening, heard the screeching of a bomb through the air. He threw himself flat on the ground, and was so stunned by a shower of incendiary bombs.

One of them rolled almost under him, and the front of his overcoat was burned away before he could scramble to his feet.

"Graziani to Duce—British Tanks Won"

MARSHAL GRAZIANI, Italian Commander-in-Chief in North Africa, has "explained" to Mussolini why his forces are being routed. He says it is "crushing superiority of British mechanised forces."

He describes the Battle of Sidi Barani as "Britain's initial success."

In his report to Mussolini he puts great emphasis on the overwhelming strength of the British forces, "constituting the best troops drawn from four continents."

The attack launched at dawn on December 9, he says, came as no surprise to the Italian command, who learned of its imminence from a prisoner taken the previous day

"READY TO ADVANCE"

According to the official Stefani agency the report reveals that it was launched at the very moment when the air preparations to resume the advance from Sidi Barani to Mersa Matruh were on the point of completion.

These preparations had been made in spite of great difficulties owing to the inadequate state of communications between the Libyan frontier and Sidi Barani and the almost entire lack of water in the occupied zone of the desert.

At the time of the British attack the main difficulties had been overcome by the construction of a water pipe-line and a 70-mile long road from Fort Capuzzo to Sidi Barani.

The Italian forces were only awaiting the arrival of some mechanised transport from Italy before launching the long expected attack on Mersa Matruh.

AIR FORCE EXCUSE

In a reference to air activity, Marshal Graziani states that owing to adverse weather conditions the Italian Air Force was not in a position to make its weight.

The Stefani Agency reports "Against the pressure exerted by air troops in the desert territory over which advance is easy, and which offered no point of resistance from the tactical point of view, the enemy threw masses of armoured cars, tanks, light, and heavy arms, supported by mobile batteries and assisted by effective aerial forces.

"It is in the crushing superiority of their armoured units employed en masse that the reason of their enemy's initial success is to be found."

Marshal Graziani added "I assert categorically that I never believed the enemy to have the means to do so with such a possibility."

"Even if the number of those who were unfortunate enough to be taken prisoner is large, that ought not to cause doubt as to their bravery."

They resisted with determination to hold on until the end.

(Press Association War Special)

GREEKS TAKE TOWN AND 800 BLACKSHIRTS

The Greeks have captured Chimara on the Adriatic coast road, and have pressed on, being to-day only ...es from Valona.

Apparently they skirted Chimara, leaving a rearguard to complete the capture.

...a, the vital Italian sea ...as been much battered by R.A.F. and shelled by warships.

...stated that an entire ...on of Blackshirts consist-... 30 officers and 800 men ...taken prisoners by the ...s near Chimara.

An Athens official statement says that flags will be flown for three days because of this new success. The battalion captured is the 133rd Blackshirts.

Nurse Kept by Lone Patient

ONE of the heroines of the raid on Manchester was 26-year-old Nurse Lilian Whitelegge, who stayed in a hospital attached to a deaf and dumb institute, looking after the only patient, a girl, aged six, called Margaret Clague. They are pictured here.

There was set company to thousands of girls at Spalding Windows of a deaf and dumb institute were shattered in the raid, and were there present.

Nurse Whitelegge would not have been in the hospital but for the deaf and dumb patients. She said "I was the only patient, and I certainly had no fear. Every now and then I thought it was rather lonely, but I knew there was ...nothing were to...

There was a terrific crash and a bomb landed on soft earth a short distance away from the door of the...

BLITZ DIDN'T SCARE THEM

Nurse Lilian Whitelegge and her patient Margaret Clague.

NURSES SAVE ALL PATIENTS

THE wing of a hospital was hit in the Manchester raid last night, and badly damaged. A birds-eye-view ...bomb dropped in the grounds ...and ...another ...which shattered the windows.

Patients in the wing affected were all removed and taken ...other ...splinter, but not seriously injured.

...patient in the wing was injured, and that there was no panic.

In another residential district where damage to private houses has been extensive a woman gave birth to a baby. An A.F.S. man and warden gave her first-aid and she was later taken to hospital.

✚ Turn to Back Page

Firewatchers Warning

WARNING to occupiers of buildings who do not employ fire-watchers was issued this afternoon by Sir Harry Haig, North-West Regional Commissioner.

Appealing for co-operation with the responsible authorities in Manchester and district, Sir Harry stated: "The idle curiosity of sight-seers hinders the operation of vital civil defence services. Do not congregate at places where the civil defence services are working.

"Those who have business in Manchester in day time should arrange, if possible, to be back in their homes before dusk. This is a great help to the transport services, and is, in addition, a wise and necessary precaution.

"It has come to my notice that certain buildings the occupiers of which are required by law to provide fire-watchers, have either had no fire-watchers, or the fire-watchers have not been functioning.

"A very serious responsibility in this matter rests with the occupiers, and if this is neglected it will be enforced most rigorously by prosecution."

German Key Town Gets Fourth Raid in a Week

Mannheim Again Left in Flames

MANNHEIM, bombed three nights in succession last week, was one of the targets in Western Germany attacked by the R.A.F. during the night. Both here and at LUDWIGSHAVEN, on the opposite bank of the Rhine, fires were started, and there were a number of explosions, the Air Ministry revealed to-day.

Bombs were dropped on Venice Lagoon during British raids on Italy on Saturday night, it was admitted in Rome to-day. As usual, they claim "neither damage nor casualties" were caused.

Other targets in the Rhineland area also bombed, says the Air Ministry. Attacks were made on the ports of FLUSHING, DUNKIRK, and CALAIS and near ...domes in channel and territory.

Chief industrial centre of the Upper Rhine, Mannheim is a key position in Germany's economic system.

BIG DOCKS

One of air aircraft is out the Docks, now heavily damaged in Docks near P.A.F. ...to be largest in the interior of German ...s those of Duisburg, Rührort, and Berlin.

Huge railway and guide yards lie at inside the docks and heavy industries and municipal works are centred there.

Foreign planes which flew over Switzerland during the night dropped four high explosive bombs and a large number of incendiaries on Zurich, causing damage in several parts of the town.

Twenty persons were injured, say the Swiss. Manchester ...at the Swiss Government said it is extending its protest to the Berlin Government against ...ing of its planes identified as British.

TWO-HOUR ALARM

The air raid track on a city ...lasted two hours and ...an air raid on several residential districts when ...dropped say the Zurich times.

The second alarm in Zurich ...lasted about an hour ...warnings at Basle a second ...time F.S. men duty ...of the town.

Nazis Admit Norway Rail Hit

...Norway state railways ...their damage to the Bergen ...was admitted...

FRONTIER REOPENED

The Franco-Italian frontier was reopened for passenger and ...traffic says a Rome message.

Bombs straddled the railway from Zurich through Winterthur to Germany, said the police, and traffic has been temporarily suspended while electric cables are being repaired.

Your Terminus

ALL Manchester Corporation transport services are at present turning back at the points where the routes are intersected by the No. 53 bus route, which runs between the Chorlton Hill Road and Old Trafford.

The authorities are endeavouring to start services at points nearer to town and a statement will be issued later in the day.

Manchester became a chief target for the German bomber planes during the war with particularly heavy raids in 1940 and 1941. A Hamburg daily newspaper reports on the success of the raid on Manchester on December 23, 1940.

The above aerial view of Manchester, probably taken before the war, was the actual map used by the German bombers to locate key targets for their bombing raids. Victoria and Central railway stations are clearly marked A and B.

On the left is the report from the Manchester Evening News of the December 23 raid. The names of places and buildings are carefully vague to avoid giving the enemy too much information and, although the attack was devastating, the emphasis in the reporting is positive -'Chins Up'-' Blitz didn't scare them' and 'Two raiders believed down'.

The camera catches the collapse of F W Woolworth & Co store at the corner of Deansgate and St Mary's Gate, December 22, 1940.

ARP men fighting the flames at a big fire at the junction of Parker Street and Portland Street. All pictures taken during the war had to be passed by the censor and none of the photographs shown here were published at the time. It was felt to be demoralising for the public . . . and would give the enemy too much information. Most of the censor's comments were hand written on the reverse of the picture — 'Banned by the censor' or 'Not to be published', and heavily underlined. Some had an official stamp like the one above.

A dramatic view across Piccadilly Gardens of the warehouses on Parker Street.

Nearly all the photographs selected are from the same two night blitz on December 22 and 23, 1940, but illustrate the horror and destruction of the time in the north west. In an age when radio and newspapers were the main source of communication, scenes like this were unknown and could only be imagined — especially as the press could not communicate the true images due to censorship. The raids continued over the years until 1944, with the last major assault on the city at Christmas. All the areas around Manchester, Salford and Stockport, where key factories were sited were affected during the raids. In Oldham a V1 attack on December 24, 1944, killed 27 people.

Fire raging in Market Street and Victoria Buildings.

Flames and smoke still pour from the bombed Exchange Station on December 23, 1940. As day breaks, a lone passer-by on his way to work at one of the factories, with his gas mask over his shoulder witnesses the destruction.
On the right, exhausted AFS and regular firemen are fighting the flames at a petroleum depot in 'a north western town'. Despite the vague nature of the proposed caption, this picture was also banned by the censor.

A direct hit on the police headquarters.

A car burns unheeded outside Chetham's Hospital on December 23, 1940, and an unharmed tandem cycle awaits its owner.

A gaping hole torn in the nurses' home at Salford Royal Infirmary, where 14 nurses were killed during an air raid on June 2. On the right is St Philip's Church from which the Rev James Hussey was walking to comfort the wounded at the hospital when he was killed by a bomb.

Workmen clearing debris after a high explosive had landed on this footpath on Wilmslow Road, Withington.

Cleaning up damage that was caused during the 1940 December 'Blitz' on Manchester. Looking across Old Market Place to the Shambles.

Ruins at Old Shambles looking from Cannon Street towards Market Street, December 22, 1940.

Bleach powder being spread along the street after a bombing.

A picture which did get past the censor and was reproduced many times. It showed the fighting spirit, good humour and stubborn courage of British citizens under fire. A group of office workers with no office left in which to work.

HRH The Duke of Kent inspecting boys of the Salford Cyclist Messengers and air raid wardens at Bexley Square, Salford, March 1941.

The Rt Hon Sir Winston Churchill with the Chief Constable of Lancaster Sir John Maxwell inspecting the bomb damage.

King George VI and Queen Elizabeth in Manchester on February 13, 1941 at the Royal Exchange.

Counting the cost

The grim scene on December 28, 1940, at Southern Cemetery, Manchester following the heaviest of the bombing raids in which 600 people from the cities of Manchester, Salford and Stockport died. A policeman stands on duty as friends and relatives of the dead pay their last respects.

At the end of the war in Europe, the MEN scored a national scoop by being the first paper to publish the great news. Realising that the end of the war was in sight, the managing editor prepared an up-to-the-minute edition every night with the giant headline "War is Over". When at last the news agency "flash" came of the Nazi capitulation on May 7, 1945, everything was ready. Within minutes, ahead of the whole country, the paper was on the streets with the news everyone had waited so long to hear. Crowds outside the MEN office eagerly scanned the papers announcing the end of the War in Europe.

VICTORY SPECIAL

Manchester Evening News

MONDAY, MAY 7, 1945 Three Halfpence

VAR IN EUROPE ENDED TO-DAY

enitz Orders "All Germans Surrender"

RMS SIGNED AT RHEIMS I.Q. OF GEN. EISENHOWER

ALL THE GERMAN FORCES HAVE SURRENDERED AND THE WAR IN EUROPE IS OVER!

It came to an end this afternoon with an announcement of total German surrender and complete Allied Victory made over the Flensburg Radio by Count von Krosigk, German Foreign Minister.

Count Krosigk was making the announcement on behalf of Admiral Doenitz, the new Führer of what is left of Germany.

The surrender was made unconditionally to the Western Allies and Russia at 2 41 a.m. (French time) to-day in the big Rheims schoolhouse which is General Dwight Eisenhower's headquarters. It was signed for Germany by Colonel-General Gustav Jodl, the new Chief of Staff of the Wermacht.

The surrender was signed for General Eisenhower by Lieut.-General Bedwell-Smith, Chief of Staff. It was also signed by General Susloparoff for Russia, and General Sevez for France.

An official Alied announcement of the surrender was then made from Rheims. Eisenhower had not been present at the signing, but he received Jodl and General-Admiral Friedburg immediately afterwards.

After signing the full surrender General Jodl was given permission to speak. "With this signature," he said, "the German people and Armed Forces are for better or worse delivered into the victors' hands."

The German-controlled Prague radio later denied the unconditional surrender report broadcast by Flensburg as far as Russia was concerned. "Only the fight against the Western Allies has ceased," said the radio.

"We Succumb"

Count von Krosigk said the surrender was ordered by Admiral Doenitz, and added: "After a heroic fight of almost six years of incomparable hardness Germany has succumbed to the overwhelming power of her enemies."

He added that to continue the war would only mean senseless bloodshed, and the collapse of all German forces had made it imperative to demand the end of hostilities.

Krosigk added: "We must accept this burden and stand loyally by our obligations. From the collapse let us save one thing—unity. No one must be under any illusions about the severity of the terms. We must face our fate."

All preparations had been made to-day for Mr. Churchill to announce the German surrender from No. 10, Downing-street.

It has been necessary to arrange the simultaneous announcement in all the Allied capitals, but the first flash of victory was all that was necessary to enable the Premier to release the news.

Balcony Hope

It was generally hoped that Mr. Churchill would at the end of this announcement address the crowd from the balcony at No. 10.

It was known that announcement by Mr. Churchill over the radio this evening would be followed by a broadcast by the King at nine o'clock.

Mr. Churchill's full-scale broadcast will come on Thursday, May 10, the fifth anniversary of his appointment as Prime Minister.

Mr. Churchill will also announce the end of the European War in the Commons, but he will make no

e ... t in ... ıll

KROSIGK said: ...en and women: ...mmand of the ...has to-day, on ...Grand-Admiral ...d the uncon... ...of all fighting

...ng Minister of ...rnment, whom ...the Fleet has ...aling with the ...n at this tragic ...tory of the ...After a heroic ... years of ...Germany ...to the over... ...of her enemies. ...the war would ...less bloodshed ...tegration.

...which has a ...ibility for the ...was compelled ...lapse of all ...forces, and ...enemy the ...

...est Task

...est task of ...Fleet and of ...porting him. ...sacrifices ...manded, to ...the war. ...number

...ended ...in ...to be ...alone. ...hour of ...and its ...of the ...Reich. ...reverence ...war

...usions"

...place the ...Our ...above all to ...bereaved, and ...struggle has

...under any ...severity of ...posed on the ...enemies. ...our fate ...ongly. ...any doubt ...difficult ...will exact ...every

"GOEBBELS' BODY FOUND IN BERLIN"

GOEBBELS'S body and those of his family have been found in an air-raid shelter near the Berlin Reichstag, according to unconfirmed reports reaching Moscow.

Many explanations have been offered to account for the disappearance of Goebbels. One of the latest, which fits in with the report of the finding of his body, is that he perished in a suicide pact with his wife and his entire family.

THE GREAT DAY

TATTOO

How News Reached the Crowds

THIS country first learned the news of the full German surrender from the Stop Press announcements in the evening papers, and then by a B.B.C. announcement at 3 p.m.

The B.B.C. said: "Here in London there is growing expectation that Mr. Churchill will broadcast to the nation in a matter of hours.

"The actual time of his victory announcement may depend on telephone talks that have been going on between London, Washington, and Moscow."

Listeners to the B.B.C. were reminded to-day that the King will broadcast at 9 p.m. on the day Mr. Churchill announces the end of the war in Europe.

Crowds of people thronged Whitehall waiting for the expected announcement and a painter was busy completing a notice in yellow paint containing three words—"War against Japan."

V(E)-Day's Court Cases Adjourned

All summonses due for hearing at Salford Magistrates' Court on V(E)-Day and V(E)-Day Plus One will be automatically adjourned a week and all persons due to appear on bail will have their bail extended for a week.

The court will sit as usual to deal with overnight prisoners, and will also deal with any case if especially asked to.

"Lord Haw-Haw" *Not* in Dublin

Reports that "Lord Haw-Haw" was one of the occupants of the German plane which landed at Gormanstown, near Dublin, on Saturday, are untrue.

British Push South From Rangoon

British troops, leaving units to mop-up in Rangoon, are pushing south from the city in heavy pre-monsoon rains.

In the oil regions Yenanama, 27 miles south of Minbu, has fallen.—Reuter.

No News Of King Leopold

Government officials in Brussels said to-day that they had no further news concerning King Leopold.

Court circles have received these tidings with some disquietude.

THE POLICE STAND BY—JUST IN CASE

METROPOLITAN policemen were standing by to-day in readiness for the expected announcement that the war had ended to deal with the crowds of revellers expected to converge of hundreds of men who can be rushed to any spot where the situation might show signs of getting out of hand.

The police will take drastic action against revellers only if

Only if a person is incapable or unruly will he be taken into "protective custody."

No special arrangements have been made for controlling the crowds in Manchester I was told

After the war is over . . .

Victory over Japan, VJ Day, August 15, 1945. The dropping of the atomic bomb on Hiroshima and Nagasaki brought the end to World War II. Four ladies from Higher Openshaw found their wartime holiday in Blackpool had become a peace celebration.

More celebrations and the demand for fireworks, even after six years of gunfire, bomb explosions, landmines and V-rockets was as great as ever. People queue for whatever fireworks were available at this Urmston shop.

The City Police band play in Albert Square to a small, damp, but happy crowd. Round the Albert Memorial a large hoarding announces a Manchester and District Exhibition to plan and rebuild the city.

On May 23, 1945, the Coalition Government which had brought the war in Europe to a successful conclusion came to an end. The General Election was set for July 5 with the counting of votes delayed until July 26 so that the Service votes could be added. The result was a landslide for Labour. This amazing picture above and the close up of the car below were taken on June 25, 1945, during Winston Churchill's campaign. His motorcade is actually crossing Mosley Street from York Street and almost completely swamped by the crowd which packed both Mosley Street and overflowed on to the area of devasation now occupied by Piccadilly Plaza.

LATE NIGHT FINAL

Manchester Evening News

ROYAL WEDDING
SOUVENIR

THURSDAY, NOV. 20, 1947.
24,466.   Three Halfpence.

eering Crowd Breaks into Palace Courtyard

ORLD HEARS RADIANT PRINCESS SAY "I WILL"

OVER 2,000 CASUALTIES

LIONS throughout the world, listening by their radio sets, heard to-day
the shy, whispered " I will " of Princess Elizabeth as the Archbishop of
Canterbury asked her in the golden blaze of Westminster Abbey:
th Alexandra Mary, wilt thou take this man to thy wedded husband ? "

p, confident tone of her bridegroom, the
nburgh, contrasted to the quiet responses of
but both were clearly heard in the Abbey
vast unseen audience.   The Duke was
mply as " Philip."

y phrase the bridegroom repeated after the
the declaration plighting troth " to love and
Momentarily their hands were unclasped.
ey were rejoined, with this difference, that
s was holding her bridegroom's hand.

ming Archbishop, with the words " with this
wed," brought to fe a sound picture of the

was an unforgettable one for the congregation
s and Queens, soldiers in khaki, admirals in
choir boys in white and scarlet, the children of
Royal in gold and crimson, prelates in their robes,
s in their turbans, and Ambassadors with multi-
ns of foreign orders slashed across their breasts.

kling Fanfare of Trumpets

d watched breathlessly as the brilliant ceremony
the West door the bride was joined by her eight
and the two pages.   Trumpeters in blue and gold
nded a sparkling fanfare as she walked slowly
great Gothic door.

s obvious that the two little pages—Prince
Gloucester and Prince Michael of Kent—in
, were having great difficulty with her train.
egroom repeatedly looked back to see how they
anaging, and to help them he deliberately slowed
s bride and himself. The King, standing on his
t as she moved to the altar, stooped down to
n for a few moments and so help the pages.
on her father's arm with her pages and brides-
ng and preceded by singing choirboys in white
he walked in procession along the six-feet wide
t laid along the whole length of nave and choir.
ke joined her at the foot of the sanctuary steps.
at each other.

nd bridegroom were together in the centre of a
ur, with the King on his daughter's left and the
n the bridegroom's right.

h of Westminster (Dr. Alan Don) in cope of
read the exhortation from the Prayer Book
ved we are gathered together here in the sight

Archbishop of Canterbury (Dr. G. F. Fisher), in
pe of white and gold brocade, performed the
ge service.

declared the bridegroom.   The words were
by the Princess.

" she said softly, when the Archbishop asked
beth Alexandra Mary, wilt thou have this man
ded husband ? "

placed a ring of Welsh gold on the Princess's
r.   Then came blessings from the Archbishop
idegroom, accompanied by Princess Margaret
pages, went up the sanctuary steps to kneel a
ar, and the King moved to his seat in the
side the Queen

er Signed in the Chapel

nging ended, bride and bridegroom, the King
Queen Mary, Princess Margaret, Princess
reece, and the two pages, with the Archbishop
y, and the Precentor of the Abbey (the Rev
n the rear left the sanctuary by a door at the
ltar and went into the Chapel of Edward the
the signing of the register and other books
bbey for such royal occasions.

d and final fanfare from the trumpeters
that the signing had been completed. With the
dering out the stirring chords of Mendelssohn's
arch the newly-married Princess and her sailor
alked slowly through choir and nave to the

idal pair passed the King and Queen, the brid-
and Princess Elizabeth dropped a deep curtsy.
pages fell over in the Abbey as the bridal
de its way to the vestry.

y bells rang out as Princess Elizabeth and her
ked towards the West door of the Abbey. The
ling happily, waved to the cheering multitudes
y her husband she entered the Glass Coach and
the Palace, acclaimed wildly all the way.
ss Elizabeth Duchess of Edinburgh and her
ned to the Palace waving, saluting, and smiling,
ng even happier than when she left. Both were

Picture the World Has Waited For
THE HAPPY COUPLE

HERE is the happiest
picture of the great
occasion—the picture
that every married
couple, of whatever

estate, treasures most.
The ceremony is over,
and now the happy
couple leave together
hand-in-hand.

Pages 2 and 3:
FULL DESCRIPTION

Pages 4, 5 and Back Page:
PHOTOGRAPHS

City Sends Its Greetings

ALDERMAN MISS MARY
KINGSMILL JONES, Lord
Mayor of Manchester, sent this
telegram to Princess Elizabeth
" On this joyful occasion citizens

Royal Highness a loyal and
heartfelt message of deep affec-
tion and wish for Your Royal
Highness and His Royal Highness the Duke of Edinburgh all
possible happiness for

On the previous page we reprint a special MEN edition of November 20, 1947, which celebrated the wedding of Princess Elizabeth to the Duke of Edinburgh.

Two years later on March 30, 1949 the Princess, accompanied by her husband the Duke of Edinburgh is being conducted on an inspection of the guard of honour of the Eighth Ardwick Battalion (Manchester Regiment) TA by Lieutentant Colonel R D Martin-Bird in Albert Square, Manchester. In the background is the Duke of Edinburgh.

The same day Princess Elizabeth visited New Cross flats, Hulme, Manchester where she was presented with a bouquet of flowers by Elsie Paine. The Princess was shown round one of the flats and when she came out she was smiling. When the Lord Mayor Dame Mary Kingsmill-Jones asked if something had amused her, the Princess replied that the old lady had called her 'luv' — a northern term of endearment.

In 1949 the last of the old trams was seen on the streets of Manchester.

. . . here are the crews who had served on the number 1007.

The London newspaper strike, March, 1955. With no newspapers in London for six days in succession, the provincial papers were in great demand, and here we see a queue of people outside the Fleet Street office of the Manchester Guardian and the Manchester Evening News waiting to buy a paper.

From the mid 50s to the early 60s there was considerable unrest at Manchester Docks which resulted in a number of strikes. Dockers here are voting to take strike action.

The picture on the left show crowds milling around outside the Manchester Evening News office to see the latest election results on October 25, 1951. The Conservatives won the election by a small majority.

Strike pickets wait outside the dock gates.

A lone policemen stands watch on Manchester's deserted dockside.

Sentinel cranes, 'frozen' by a protest strike, mark the silent skyline beyond during one of the 50s
dockyard strikes.

While the country's shipbuilding yards lie silent, all is bustle and normal activity in the Manchester docks during the 1957 strike. This
picture shows number nine dock where ships are busy loading, unloading and accepting freight. The only part of Manchester docks
affected by the great strike is the dry dock. On the right the merchant ships move up and down the Ship Canal as usual, helping to keep
the country's exports flowing.

Britain's first-ever bomber, the historic Avro 504 Biplane, was rebuilt by four veteran craftsmen who had worked on the original 504 production lines during the first world war. The biplane was built specially to take part in the film of the life of legless fighter ace Group Captain Douglas Bader who learned to fly in an Avro 504.

A Lancaster Bomber, brought out of storage for the Associated British Picture Corporation's film 'The Dam Busters' starring Richard Todd as Guy Gibson, VC, and Michael Redgrave as Dr Barnes Wallis, the man who invented the bombs which blew the dams in Germany during World War II.

You never know who you might meet in Manchester. In 1958 Cary Grant chats to a student in St Peter's Square during his surprise tour of the city prior to a personal appearance at the Theatre Royal.

Danny Kaye the uncrowned king of entertainers held court in a Manchester hotel in 1974, prior to conducting the Hallé orchestra at the Free Trade Hall. The visit fulfils a promise made 15 years previously to Sir John Barbirolli that he would one day conduct the orchestra in Manchester. His twelve thousand mile round trip from California was arranged by the Variety Club of Great Britain, with the aim to raise money for handicapped and under-privileged children in the north west.

The world's first successful stored-programme computer was another Manchester University first and built by professors Fred Williams and Tom Kilburn, aided by engineer Geoff Toothill. It ran its first programme in 1948 with a memory capacity of thirty two words, but until this breakthrough computers had been just calculating machines.

1958 and the famous picture of Jodrell Bank in Cheshire by Tom Stuttard at the time of the first moon landing by the Russian Sputnik 1. Jodrell Bank, now a popular tourist attraction, was the creation of Professor Sir Bernard Lovell of Manchester University.

September 8, 1957, and the fire at Pauldens Department Store which completely gutted this famous retail outlet in Stretford Road, All Saints. The fire began on the first floor in the early evening and in less that three hours the building was completely gutted. More than twenty fire fighting appliances were at the scene. The remains are seen here still smouldering the following day.

. . . and a fast forward to 1969 with this dramatic picture of a double-decker bus which had crashed through the road at the site of the Pauldens fire.

Disaster at Wythenshawe

On March 14, 1957, a BEA Airliner crashed into houses at the end of the runway at Manchester's Ringway airport. Squads of firemen toiled over redhot brickwork and smouldering timber in the search for a woman and child missing in one of the houses. All 20 occupants of the plane - 15 passengers and five crew - plus the Wythenshawe woman and her son died in the crash. The plane, flagship of the Discovery class of Viscounts, was on flight from Amsterdam and overshot the runway while coming in to land.

The appalling disaster highlighted the concern of all residents living in close proximity to the airport.

The end of the runway after the Viscount air disaster in Wythenshawe in 1957. Smoke still obscures the houses demolished by the aircraft as the rescue operation continues and officials in the foreground search the ground for clues to the crash.

Munich

Manchester United party pictured as they left Ringway Airport on the ill-fated airliner which crashed at Munich. From the left: Jackie Blanchflower, Bill Foulkes, Walter Crickmer secretary, Manchester Guardian journalist Don Davies, Roger Byrne captain, Duncan Edwards, Albert Scanlon, Frank Swift, Ray Wood, Dennis Viollet, journalist Archie Ledbrook, Jeff Bent, Mark Jones, journalist Alf Clarke.

DAVID MEEK — was a young journalist at the time of the Munich crash.

A large part of Manchester eats, sleeps and talks sport, especially football, and in particular Manchester United and Manchester City.

It's why the sports department of the Manchester Evening News makes soccer a priority with four specialist reporters concentrating on the clubs in the area of Greater Manchester.

Paul Hince followed Peter Gardner as the man writing about Manchester City while I count it my good fortune to have been the Manchester United correspondent for the last 35 years.

As you might gather from that length of stint, it is not a job you easily walk away from, and I am not alone in that respect. My predecessor, the much respected and well-liked Tom Jackson, had represented the paper at Old Trafford for 25 years before becoming one of the eight journalists killed in the Munich air crash of 1958.

Indeed, looking back through the archives it might well be that there have only been four regular correspondents specialising in Manchester United since the club was formed in 1878.

The Manchester Evening News has long recognised the importance of United and City in the hearts of its readers which is why in 1958 they switched their leader writer from politics to sport to cover the tragedy of Munich.

Manchester virtually came to a stop when the news of the terrible accident at Munich reached the city. The first flashes were wired into the Evening News offices and the Editor, Tom Henry, immediately produced a special edition.

People waited outside the office for the latest reports as word spread of the worst tragedy in the history of English football as the team were flying home after a European Cup tie against Red Star Belgrade and made a refuelling stop at Munich.

It was an anguished way to start a career as Manchester United correspondent. It was also meant to be a temporary appointment, but there never seems to have been sufficient of a lull in the flow of news from Old Trafford to consider my assignment completed.

Manchester Evening News
LATE FINAL
27,654 TV & RADIO—PAGE 2 THURSDAY, FEBRUARY 6, 1958 PRICE 3d.

Phone your news … NEWS DESK. Tel. …

UNITED CUP XI CRASH: "28 DIE"

Plunged into houses at Munich, exploded

SURVIVORS SAVED in BLAZING WRECKAGE

ONE of the greatest disasters to befall British football struck Manchester United this afternoon when the plane carrying the £350,000 wonder team crashed at Munich. At least 28 of the 40 aboard were killed; some reports said higher casualties were feared.

The "Elizabethan" airliner.

The plane, a B.E.A. Elizabethan, had just taken off and climbed to 60ft. when it crashed on the outskirts of the city.

The team was returning from Belgrade, where yesterday United drew 3-3 with Red Star, the Yugoslav champions, and so qualified for the semi-final of the European Cup.

The plane came down in the suburb of Kirchtrudering, exploding as it hit the ground. Several houses were set on fire.

Confirmation of fears that 28 had died seemed to come in a B.E.A. statement at Munich that there were 12 survivors.

But the position was confused when another report said the number on board was not 40 but 38 passengers and six crew.

Pulled from blazing wreck

It was also stated that the scene of the crash was Riem, a village near Munich airport.

THEN a B.E.A. spokesman said at least 10 to 15 people were pulled alive from the blazing wreckage.

The plane had landed at Munich from Belgrade for refuelling.

It is not yet known whether any local inhabitants were injured in the crash.

The plane had been due to reach Ringway, Manchester, at 5 p.m. to-day.

Ministry inspector flies out

The crash had happened at 3 10 p.m. Within an hour the Ministry of Transport and Civil Aviation in London said Mr. G. M. Kelly, an inspector of accidents, was leaving immediately for Munich.

As he prepared to leave, it was learned that the crash had occurred in a snowstorm.

One unconfirmed eye-witness report said 16 badly-burned bodies were recovered from the wrecked airliner.

The Munich B.E.A. office promised a full statement on the accident with an hour.

On hearing of the crash, Mr. Alan Hardaker, Football League secretary, contacted League president Joe Richards, of Barnsley, and the Wolverhampton club, who are due to play United on Saturday.

Manchester's Lord Mayor, Alderman Leslie Lever, said: "I am very deeply grieved to hear about this tragic accident, and I am sure that everyone in Manchester and beyond will feel the same."

Football officials were trying to notify Sir Stanley Rous, F.A. secretary. They hoped to reach him in Edinburgh before he flew back to London to-night.

And **BACK IN MUNICH** fire brigades which had sped to the scene were battling with flames which had fired two buildings.

United players and other members of the party boarding the ill-fated airliner at Ringway on Monday. In the group are Walter Crickmer (secretary), Frank Swift, Scanlon, Wood, Viollet, Archie Ledbrooke, Bent, Whelan, Jones, Gregg, and Morgans.

Sport's biggest tragedy

THIS air crash is the greatest blow British sport has ever suffered.

Because when that plane crashed on take-off from Munich airport it wrecked the lives of so many members of a team which had been flying the flag for our soccer.

From the ashes of the old prewar poverty-stricken Manchester United they had lifted the team sky-high to world fame and were cruising towards the greatest soccer treble history has known.

But Fate stepped in with all its unexpectedness and viciousness. And struck the greatest blow at what the world has become to recognise the greatest club.

It was a team which carried transfer market value of more than £250,000, according to present-day values.

CUP THREAT

And, furthermore, this unfortunate crash could also wreck the European Cup competition and turn the heads of all clubs against flying to and from matches.

League champions and Cup runners-up, United were on their way home from their great Cup triumph against Red Star, Yugoslavia, in Belgrade yesterday. They had halted at Munich for a break. Then took off again and misfortune stepped in. . . .

Stepped in with dramatic suddenness to throw up a doubt also about the staging of Saturday's First Division game with Wolves at Old Trafford.

Matt Busby, the man who built this United from a struggling pre-war unit into such a terrific monument to soccer was with them. So also was Tom Curry the trainer, and Bert Whalley the coach.

EDUCATION MAN DIES

Former senior official in Manchester's education department, Mr. James Henry Torbitt, has died in his Mansfield, Notts, home, aged 82.

MATT BUSBY

The Busby genius

MATT BUSBY started his career in a quiet way with Denny Hibernians, a little-known Scottish club. When Manchester City brought him south he was struggling, until suddenly switched to wing-half. Then he blossomed, won a Scottish "cap," and was transferred to Liverpool.

Came th ewar. He went into khaki, became a sergeant, and travelled Europe with Army teams. On his return, Manchester United invited him to take over their vacant post of manager, and he began his long job of building up the fortunes of the Old Trafford club.

He tock them to three League championships, a winning Cup-final in 1948, and to Wembley again last May.

Twelve months ago they reached the semi-final of the European Cup, as they had done by beating Yugoslavia Red Star in Belgrade 24 hours ago.

Of firm, but quiet disposition, Matt was a slow-speaking Scot with a delightfully warm character.

A killer's plea

Albert Edward Matheson, aged 52, sentenced to death for murdering a 15-year-old boy at Newcastle, is appealing against the sentence.

WAS V.I.P. BABY ON THE PLANE?

Mrs. Vera Ludic (pictured here) wife of the Yugoslav air attache in London, and her 22-month-old daughter, may have been on the plane.

When the United party left Manchester Airport, Mrs. Lukic, aged 24, went with them.

She was going to collect her daughter from her parents' home in Belgrade and also to watch the European Cup match.

Then she and the child were to fly home with United.

Dentists: 'Pay is down one third'

SINCE 1948, dentists' earnings have dropped by about one-third, the Royal Commission on doctors' and dentists' pay was told in London to-day.

Dentists blamed scales of charges and administration for "restricting work to a stereo-typed pattern and cutting down fees."

BRIGHTON CONSPIRACY TRIAL

Bennett shouts: I didn't swindle tax

DRAMA mounted in the Brighton conspiracy trial at the Old Bailey to-day as witness Allan Roy Bennett, immaculately dressed a big cigar sticking from his breast pocket, shouted replies at defence counsel.

Barristers, public, and judge listened in silence to exchanges between Bennett and Mr. Geoffrey Lawrence, Q.C., who defended the suspended chief constable.

Mr. Lawrence, his hands sometimes resting on the ledge in front of him, sometimes resting them on his hips, put every question in the same quiet, even, measured tones.

Bennett sometimes answered him in a shout, flinging his arms about, but Mr. Lawrence's next question would be put as quietly and calmly as the one which preceded it.

In cross-examination Bennett, who has admitted reporting alleged bribes to Scotland Yard . . .

- **CLAIMED** he now mixed with big people.
- **DENIED** that while owner of the Astor ("Bucket of Blood") Club at Brighton he was engaged on an income tax swindle.
- **ADMITTED** his first conviction was at **Salford** in 1931 when he was 13 and that he had been jailed at **Manchester**.
- **DISCLOSED** that one of the two names he had written on a piece of paper as those who had informed him that Brighton police had been crooked was Tony Lyons

The piece of paper was Exhibit 48 in the drama.

Six hours

Bennett ended his evidence after being in the box six hours.

Accused are: Charles Field Williams Ridge, aged 58, of Bavant Road, Brighton, suspended chief constable of the town; Detec.-Inspec. John Richard Hammersley, aged 40 (second-in-command of Brighton C.I.D. until he was suspended), of Glen Rise, Withdean, Brighton; Detec.-Sgt. Trevor Ernest Heath, aged 36, of Bramble Rise, Withdean, also suspended; Anthony John Lyons, aged 59, licensee, of Marine Gate, Brighton; and Samuel Bellson, aged 42, commission agent, of The Drive, Hove.

They have pleaded not guilty to conspiring together and with persons unknown to obstruct the course of public justice.

Bennett was to-day first questioned by **Mr. David Peck** (for Hammersley) about an interview in Hammersley's office when Heath was present.

He said he was indignant when Heath inquired about a "job" at Bournemouth. "I told him it was all nonsense."

He did not know whether he said: "If I am called in every time a screwing job is done something will have to be done about it."

Cash book

Bennett was then cross-examined by **Mr. Stanley Rees** (for Lyons) about the cash book relating to the Astor Club.

Q: When you were living honest and upright life you took £60 a week out of the club takings and omitted it from the books?—**YES.**

Bennett, waving his arms, said: "Could I declare £20 a week to Ridge on the books? Could I put down: Chief Constable, £20 a week?"

Q.: I am not permitted to answer questions. I realise you are perhaps having a difficult time.—**I am not having a difficult time. I admit I took £60 a week, £20 for Ridge and £40 for me, and I admit I did not pay tax on it.**

Mr. Rees: You may make any admission you are moved to do, but for the moment will you just answer these questions.

'Another fraud'

Bennett said he had made an income-tax return at the end of 1955 and for all the years prior to that, but had not made out one since.

He agreed, therefore, that he had never returned his income for 1955

Mr. Rees: Because of course, you were engaged in a swindle:

Fuchs—Serious trouble

DR. FUCHS was reported to-night to be in serious trouble about 28 miles south of Depot 700 on his trek from the South Pole.

Two Snocats in Dr. Fuchs's party were reported to have dropped into crevasses. Both were recovered, but the steering of one was broken.

Dr. Fuchs was off the course made by Sir Edmund Hillary on his trek to the Pole late last year and was trying to find his way back.

CHEERS!

Building of a new Hale public-house, the Moss Hotel, may start this summer.

Jockey Joe Childs dies

OLD-TIME jockey Joe Childs, who for 10 years was first jockey to King George V, has died at Portsmouth, aged 73.

Born in France, he joined the British Army in World War I—and so made his name in England.

In 1916, while on leave, he won the substitute Derby and Oaks, run at Newmarket, on Fifinella.

Two years later, on Gainsborough, he won the 2,000 Guineas, the substitute Derby, and the St. Leger.

He was perhaps the finest exponent of waiting tactics. He retired in 1935.

Other classic successes were: On Coronach in the Derby of 1926; Scuttle (1928) and Brown Betty (1933) in the 1,000 Guineas; Cameronian (1931) in the 2,000 Guineas; Bayuda (1919) and Love in Idleness (1921) in the Oaks; and four St. Leger winners in Hurry On (1916), Polemarch (1921), Solario (1925), and Coronach (1926).

"Evil of teenage girls drinking . . ."

Police action was threatened to-day to clamp down on after-time drinking at Oldham clubs.

And the "evil" of teenage girls drinking could be removed by the vigilance of licensees, said Police Chief Mr. W Schofield.

ORGANIST MOVES

After 10 years as organist and choirmaster at St. Alban's Church, Offerton, Stockport, Mr. N. B. Hunter moves to Sacred Trinity Church, Salford.

12 buses join ice-skid toll

EVENING NEWS REPORTER

SNOW dusted the North-West with danger to-day when light showers frozen over roads, causing dozens of skid-and-bump accidents.

Many people were late for work through road hold-ups which delayed some buses up to half an hour.

And with more snow or sleet showers on the way and the temperature not expected to rise much over freezing point, motorists were urged to take great care when going home to-night.

Manchester Corporation Transport Department had about 12 buses in minor accidents There were delays averaging 15 minutes on many services.

Most rail services were not affected and air traffic from Manchester Airport was trouble-free. But those roads. . . .

One of the worst crawls was on the Stockport-Manchester road. Long queues formed and it took some buses 25 minutes to get from Ardwick Green to Deansgate.

FREAK FREEZE-UPS

Loads of salt were tipped on the ice-bound junction of Prince's Bridge and Water-street, Salford—but not until after there had been three crashes and several cases of skidding.

Passengers dodged flying glass when a lorry side-skidded in Medlock-street, Hulme. One passenger was treated for shock.

In Chester Road a bus and car bumped together—and 100 yards away a car and motor-cyclist crashed at the same time.

Freak freeze-ups made some roads more dangerous than others.

LORRIES CRASH

There was a heavy snow shower in Ashton-under-Lyne this afternoon and a flurry of big flakes in Manchester.

CIRCLED.—A lorry in Hyde Road, West Gorton, Manchester went round in a circle and cut a telephone pole in half.

LAST WORDS. — And there's a silver lining There will be another frost to-night, but to-morrow should be a little warmer.

31 strike at pit over pay

LATE FLASH.—Over a pay dispute 31 colliers at Bradford Pit, Manchester, struck to-day.

PIT union secretary Mr. Jack Collins is to "defend not condemn" miners summoned to the first "absentee court" at Dairy Colliery, Haigh, near Wigan, next week.

He said to-day: "A lot of people are getting it into their heads that union members are going to condemn their own men."

Mr. Collins said the 350 miners at the pit had "their backs up a bit" at being called a "guinea-pig" in the new drive to cut absentism. "Courts" had already been held in some collieries.

Two pit strikes ended to-day. They were at:

- **Wheatsheaf**, Pendlebury, near Manchester, where 170 night-shift men wanted to swap with day workers;
- **Wigan Junction**, Platt Bridge, near Wigan, where hauliers staged a "revenge" strike after colliers struck. Talks have started to try to settle both these disputes.

Man drops 20ft.—glass saves him

EVENING NEWS REPORTER

WINDOW cleaner Edward Clayton, aged 23, of College Buildings, Collyhurst, Manchester, escaped death by inches when he fell from the top floor of the All Saints' Register Office building, Manchester.

After plunging 20ft. he crashed through the glass roof of a corridor over a courtyard.

Witnesses said: "If it hadn't broken his fall the window cleaner almost certainly would have been killed."

A few inches either way and he would have carried on falling another 20 or 30 feet to the concrete well below.

FLYING BAN LIFTED LAST YEAR

THE Football League banned teams flying to and from matches after the whole Turin team was wiped out on March 4, 1949, when their plane hit Turin Cathedral in a storm.

THE LEAGUE LIFTED THE BAN ON CLUBS FLYING ONLY LAST MARCH.

The F.A. has never banned teams flying abroad, but last March gave permission for clubs to fly only for League matches in England and Wales.

At Llandow, South Wales, in March, 1950, 80 died when a plane bringing supporters from the Ireland v. Wales Rugby International crashed.

Missing boy is in Ireland

FOURTEEN-YEAR-OLD Anthony Haslam, missing from Macclesfield for a week, has been found in County Cavan, Ireland

Anthony, of Wilwick Lane, was found with a friend, Michael Wadsworth, aged 17, of Western Avenue, Macclesfield. They were staying with Wadsworth's grandmother.

Two painters dangle 30ft. up

EVENING NEWS REPORTER

TWO painters clung to ropes 30ft. up when the safety hooks of their cradle failed while they worked on a warehouse wall in Brazil-street, in Manchester's centre, this afternoon.

A fire engine rescued the men.

A spokesman of the men's employers said: "They were never in any danger. They grasped the ropes as a precaution and were soon lowered to the ground."

One of the painters said: "Please don't print my name. My wife would be worried stiff she thinks I work on the ground."

Eoka's threat

Greek Cypriots to-day gave notice to Sir Hugh Foot that they would continue the Cyprus struggle. "Our patience is exhausted," said Eoka leaflets.—Reuter.

ON HIS WAY

Disturbed by the occupants after breaking into a house called By the Way, in Yew Tree Lane, Northenden, Manchester, a raider fled empty-handed.

1 H

PEOP… KILLED… HOM…

… and Whelan for L…

2 I

ON BOA…

… Clarke ("Evening …

3 H

Councillor Edw… Mayor of Stretfor… long United supp… "Millions of … thro… world …

None of the Uni… was in the plane, … go on the trip to B…

Mr. Harold H… chairman, said: "… tragedy—knock out all."

4 O

COMMONS …

SUICIDE.—No … on suicide.—Mr. B…

POOLS.—No le… permit subscription… pools in cash.

TROOPING.—Tro… rehearsals on Satu…

MURDERS. — I… and December 195… in England and Wa… with … same peri… Butler.

WITHDRAWN.—… Police withdrawn … prints be taken of … charged with mino… Mr. Butler.

ARMED ROB… authority to give … courts on nature … they imposed.—Mr. …

Condition of the … Agriculture, Mr. Jo… has bronchitis, "a…

The ill-fated Elizabethan airliner in flames at Munich.

Bill Foulkes, one of the few survivors, is pictured amidst the wreckage at the scene of the crash.

A spectacular collapse of Barton Bridge during its construction in 1959. Officials survey the damage before the canal below can be re-opened.

Belle Vue . . . and after the great fire of 1958 this is all that remained of the York Restaurant and the popular Coronation Ballroom.

The world's longest-running peak time drama series was started by Granada Television on December 9, 1960. Who was to guess that the homely scenes from Manchester and Salford would be viewed all over the world? Here, in the back room of the Rover's Return - the 'snug', Minnie Caldwell gets another telling off from Ena Sharples while Martha Longhurst concentrates on her milk stout. The landlord, Jack Walker, looks on.

Another popular character in Coronation Street Elsie Tanner (centre) at her marriage to Steve the US Airman surrounded by friends and neighbours from the series.

On this page you can see the sequence of events following the de-railment and crash of a school excursion train carrying nearly 250 children from Staffordshire to York. The accident happened at Cheadle Hulme station and these are a few of the contact prints from a cameraman at the scene of the crash. The picture editor would select one or more photographs to illustrate the reporter's copy, and you can see in the front page opposite how the contact picture in the middle of the second row has been used to fit the page layout.

LATE FINAL Edition

ON THE DAWES PLAN

Manchester Evening News
and Chronicle

Biggest sale in Provinces

TWICE THE CHOICE

LOOKERS OF MANCHESTER

THURSDAY, MAY 28, 1964   29,516   PRICE 4d

Phone news and picture ideas to NEWS DESK. Tel. BLA 2345.

ngsters join in songs | *Comics and sweets lie* | *Trapped boy hero asks*
forget the horror | *strewn on wrecked line* | *about other children*

CHOOL OUTING SPECIAL
RASHES ON RAIL BRIDGE

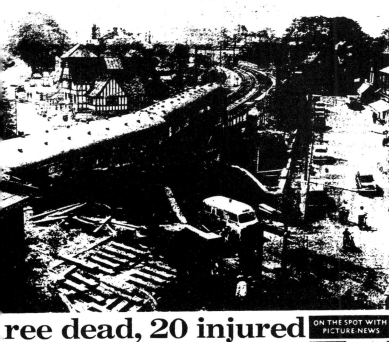

Scenes of chaos at Cheadle Hulme Station after the crash

● Pictures by staff photographers Eric Graham, Clive Cooksey, and John Featherstone. More pictures Page 10.

ON THE SPOT WITH PICTURE-NEWS

Safe in his arms

The strong arms of an ambulance man comfort this little girl passenger, who collapsed with shock after the crash.

ree dead, 20 injured
coaches keel over

y a special team of "Evening News" Reporters

people were killed and 20 injured, four seriously, when a l excursion train ran off the rails in a few nightmare seconds at Hulme Station today. People watched in horror as the train, from Gnosall, Staffs, carrying nearly 250 children on a sightseeing trip to York, broke up.

The victims were an eight-year-old girl, 12-year-old Lewis Stevens, and Mr M Pedley, a railway representative from Burton-on-Trent, who was travelling with the party.

Badly injured children were thrown on the track, a carriage plunged on its side, and a railway bridge over Station Road, Cheadle Hulme, was partly demolished.

The crash occurred as the train approached the station. Sandwiches, sweets, and comics lay strewn among the tangled tracks.

Cheshire emergency services went into immediate action. Ambulances took the injured to Stockport infirmary where doctors were standing by to give emergency operations, rest centres were set up around the disaster scene for the children who escaped unhurt, and the wreckage was searched for trapped survivors.

Hours after the disaster officials were still amazed that there were virtually few casualties. One railway official said: "It is nothing short of a miracle. When you look at the damage to the carriages it is hard to believe that so many got out uninjured."

The bridge was being widened by railway engineers. It was part of a plan to give the station a face-lift. Excavation and pile-driving had been going on around it for months.

"I comforted her"

A private inquiry into the disaster will be held by Mr Tom Chapelhow, divisional operating superintendent for the Manchester Division, at Hunts Bank, Manchester, on Monday. There will be no statement after this meeting, but a full Ministry of Transport inquiry will follow.

The driver of the train was Mr Malcolm Charles Smith, of Stafford, and his fireman was Mr J. Gillyett, also of Stafford, a Hindu, recently married.

Many eyewitnesses kept appearing as they told of the first scenes after the crash, which happened at about 9.40 am. A baby's injured 10-year-old girl helped to effect the rescue. Mr Donald Dimler, a business of Swann Lane, Cheadle Hulme, said: "Am I dreaming? It must be a dream."

Mr Pimlott said: "She was dreadfully conscious. I talked to her for comfort her."

The children were from schools in the Stone and Stafford areas. They had been saving up for the trip to see long Minster.

The crash happened at the junction of the Manchester Crewe and Manchester-Macclesfield lines, blocking them both. Mr Andrew Murray, of Vicarage Avenue, Cheadle Hulme, saw the whole horror.

"One of the carriages suddenly began to rock. It went on rocking and then rolled over on its side with a deafening crash. It was dragged on by the train and then the carriages behind it fell away hitting the bridge and platform.

"More than 20 ambulances raced to the scene. Teams of firemen, doctors and nurses used lifting gear and hacksaws still attached to the coaches."

Split in half

But a fireman said: "We don't know how many are in there." This coach had been dragged about 100 yards from

---

---

will be out of n for two days

Rush-hour passengers to Bramhall will be met this evening by a bus at Hazel Grove, and other bus services are being arranged for Poynton, Adlington, and Prestbury.

Traffic to Crewe was being diverted via the Styal loop.

British Railways said later that both main lines to London from Manchester via Crewe and Stoke were blocked.

It was hoped to have the Crewe line back in operation later this evening.

Rescue drama

five wrecked carriages leaning at crazy angles and the station platform completely shattered.

one carriage remained on the sagging temporary bridge over Station Road.

Mr David Rogers, of Ladybrook Road, Bramhall, was in his car on the road when masonry from the bridge fell in front of him.

He said: "Just before I had heard a screech which ended in brakes and was the train swaying. The next thing I knew beams and bits of masonry came raining down in front of me.

"I wrenched free a passenger," said Mr Robert Rundale, manager of the Cheadle Hulme Junction Hotel.

Some of Mr Pimlott's assistants were taking in the station as far as I can see some younger children from another crush very badly hurt school in Stone.

"Some are dead."

Those who were not injured were taken to the nearby Methodist Hall where they sat in quiet groups while local housewives and social workers made tea.

- One little girl has lost a leg aged about nine, who was the last of the children to be taken from the train. He had been trapped for about an hour.

Crying

Connie Douglas Blewett, of Nicholson Avenue, Macclesfield, who helped to lift the body of the shattered carriage, said: "His left hand was badly crushed but he was talking to us very calmly. He kept asking how the others were."

The boy was thought to be John Gibson, of Greenwood Road, Stafford, later found at one of the seriously injured.

There were 246 school children in the train, mainly from the Stone area. They were from the Gnosall County Secondary School, Stafford.

RACING

YORK

Mossco 1 Ragsay 2 Bibi S.P.—11-8 (fav), 9-1, 9

TOTE DIVIDENDS

£ 30-Win £2 plat 8

8 2   Daily double 1

Dearer papers

Regional daily newspapers cost the equivalent ol an o 4d from June 1

£22M PLANT—ICI to another plant to make pelymer at cost of £22M will be alongside existing at Wilton Works, North Y shire.

RAIL CRASH
▼ (See This Page)
British Railways said person still unaccounted for Road under damaged closed to traffic, and diverting traffic. Road not re opened until coaches on above were moved.

WIFE ACQUITTED BURGLARY CHARG
Housewife Roberta Delaney (19), Newton St Gorton, acquitted at Mane Crown Court of burglary house in May Road, Whit Range, Manchester.

MAN DIES IN TRENC
Irishman killed when raised in a Maidstone, Workmate rescued uncon by firemen after being bu under tons of earth for hours.

BEEF PRICE FALLS
WHOLESALE prices Southfield M London have dropped pound since last Thu spokesman for the Tr Association said

JUDY GARLAN
(See This Page)
Radio correspondent Garland given oxyg doctors worked on h hours out of danger f critical. Nature of illn given. Miss Garland s terrified of storms. W in hotel room 90 mph w raced.

GREEKS ARRES
ARMY 4 SERGEAN
Greek Cyprjot police arr British Army sergeant in N after he refused to allow in tion of official documents.

SCOTTISH LEAGUE PL Third Lanark's proposal Scottish League should reconstructed to include second division of 16 club with five clubs dropping Third Division, defeated i votes to seven at S League annual general m in Glasgow.

JAIL—OR ARMY—Atte Recorder at West Ham in two men option of gow in army Army will be common by Labour M George Wigg

VANISHED U
MAN—CAR FOU
Car of missing Un ol Food and Agriculture o bation, Willie Ellingto found in town of Carlisl 15 miles south of Rom police. Parked not far lake side lake Kingston a 11 days ago from Rome where he lived with wife

Driver fined
Eustace Brian C life member of the 1915 and a driver for years, was fined £30 for driving at 31 in close followed by an accident Cooke's Jaguar and accid in Handforth

SEAMAN I
MERCY DAS
British seaman B S taken to hospital for prary operation in Alb bring four fingers bec hand during a storm South Aegean on a woman, a member of the missionnaire's t trapped his hand in equipment. The ship Piraeus. Athens port was taken off.

Airport a
When a Soviet air airliner tried to emergency alert London Airport tho shot the runway safely on the second

---

Hospital staff work non-stop

BY A STAFF REPORTER

TEAMS of doctors and nurses at Stockport Infirmary worked non-stop to aid the rail crash injured.

A fleet of ambulances went to the scene and by 10.30 the first ambulance arrived back at the infirmary with injured children.

Mr Edmund Durrant, the group secretary, said that a casualty staff of 30 and a team of doctors were working. They were treating the injured casualties; people were injured.

8 300 others were taken to Stockport Infirmary with injuries that were said to be of not serious.

They included Jean Wyatt aged nine of Hitworn Stafford Paul Moriarty, aged eight, Linder Bank, Stafford, Susan Answic, Stafford, Edith Mitchel Stafford and Susan Harvey, Icychenhall Mrs Kathleen Potter aged 55, of Yatxfield House near Stone, Ada Nixon aged 55 of Wanfield near Stafford, and Mrs Joan Tilsch of Stafford.

BADLY HURT

Four children seriously injured were John Gibson, aged nine, of Greenwood Road, Stafford (arm and leg injuries); Susan Meddicott aged 11 of Crompton Road, Drukey (head and leg injuries), Susan Walsh, aged 11, of Coal Avenue, Stafford (leg) and Peter Stone (ar— injury). As far as is known Driver staff in a unknown road and one unknown women.

Some were in a casualty department where the injured were taken, and others brought in.

Judy Garland in coma: 'Critical'

JUDY GARLAND was today rushed to a Hong Kong hospital unconscious and in a critical condition.

An American radio correspondent gave the news in a broadcast from Hong Kong.

Earlier, the 42-year-old singer, who was slow-handclapped in Melbourne Australia, last week, said she "hadn't a home" where she was going after Hong Kong. She were wanted to do a stage play in London.

She said the Press were "absolutely beastly" to her in Melbourne

---

In 1965 one of the world's most famous infants, the original Rolls-Royce Silver Ghost came back to its birthplace. The visit to Royce Court, Hulme was for the unveiling of a plaque recording that nearby stood the first Rolls-Royce factory where it was built in 1906.

Silent demonstrations . . . holding posters off-duty firemen from all over the north west massed outside Manchester town hall while their pay claim was discussed.

The scene in Moult Street on 30 October 1969. When a serious fire broke out in the foundry of the Manchester Evening News. Two of the 24 firemen tackling the outbreak were overcome by fumes and had to be treated at Manchester Royal Infirmary.

University of Salford. The six-storey building contains the main teaching rooms including two lecture theatres and a number of laboratories.

John Rylands famous University Library.

Manchester Museum, which adjoins part of Manchester University to the left.

Rag Day - and students from Manchester University gather on Deansgate for an unusual stunt in 1957.

Salford University boat crew led by 'stroke' Phil Stollery, prepare for the 1986 Varsity boat race against Manchester University on the Irwell.

Students from Salford University and Technical College were making a small protest as they handed out tea and biscuits to bemused drivers in an early morning traffic jam outside the University. Badges with the slogan 'I know poverty, I had breakfast with a student' were provided with the cuppa.

Scammonden Bridge — M62 1969, and just taking shape high up on the Pennine moors is a bridge which would span the 600ft gap left by blasting a route for the Lancashire-Yorkshire motorway through the wall of the Scammonden Valley. The M62 motorway was opened in 1971.

The Robin Hood railway bridge at Clifton.

The M62 has proved to be a valuable link over the Pennines, except when everyone wants to use it at once! The motorway police arrive to try to sort out this hold-up in the Irwell Valley section in 1978.

Another view of the bridge being built over the river Irwell at Clifton.

The mighty Wurlitzer organ that had entertained thousands at the Odeon Cinema is moved out of the theatre by volunteers for the Lancastrian Theatre Organ Trust. It was to be re-assembled and situated in the Free Trade Hall.

In January 1973 Earl Mountbatten attends Indian Association celebrations in Rochdale and meets Cyril Smith, MP.

The Osmond Brothers at the Free Trade Hall 1970's. 14-year-old Donny Osmond sings to screaming weeny. . boppers who came in their hundreds to worship their new idols.

Ecstatic fans at a Bay City Rollers concert held at Belle Vue, Manchester in 1975.

1977 and a new Speakers' Corner outside the Library in St Peter's Square. Here, this speaker with his assistant dressed in Pilgrim's costume is against Britain joining the European Common Market.

This shows the re-development in the Market Street area in Manchester and the site of the Arndale Centre. On the right is a photograph by Bill Bachelor of the Wellington Inn and Sinclairs Oyster Rooms together known as the Old Shambles. They were saved from demolition during the new development in an amazing building operation in 1971. The entire building was raised four foot nine and a half inches from its original street level to fit in with the new surrounding buildings. The Wellington Inn had survived for over 600 years and, as we saw earlier, had even escaped Hitler's bombs.

In 1975 public opinion won against Greater Manchester Council who wanted to turn Sackville Gardens into a construction site for the planned Picc-Vic underground rail link.

In 1981 Maggie and Chris Nolan with the help of local youngsters turned their cellar into a youth club for the children of the Collyhurst area.

Residents of Miriam Street, Bradshaw Avenue and Gail Close of Failsworth were dancing in the street when they were voted the best decorated neighbourhood for the Royal Wedding of Prince Charles and Lady Diana Spencer in July 1981

Making a grab for cakes in Coppice Close, Woodley these youngsters celebrate the wedding with another street party.

MANCHESTER EVENING NEWS **11**
Thursday September 16 1982

Council plans £½m lights, song and dance extravaganza

Super city Christmas!

Massive festive campaign to woo back the shoppers

By GERALD BROWN

MANCHESTER is set to transform itself into a magical wonderland this Christmas.

The city centre will become a riot of festive lights and tableaux in a £500,000 extravaganza, plus buskers, open-air singing and even the possibility of a traditional Chinese dragon dance.

It's all part of a long-term campaign by the city council and big business to lure thousands of shoppers back to the city.

There has been concern that over the past 15 years, Manchester has slipped from its top spot as leading trading city outside London to somewhere between 12th and 20th.

It has been hit hard by thrusting towns like Altrincham and Stockport, which have proved major attractions with free parking and new retail centres.

Coun William Egerton, leader of Manchester City Council, Lord Mayor of Manchester Coun Clifford Tomlinson, Mr Andrew Smith, vice-president of Manchester Chamber of Trade, and Mr

Maxine Burns, Christine Summerfield and Barbara Heatchcote of A H Knowles, P R, of Manchester, showing a display of goods which will be on sale to promote the city.

Cooked Meats
Prime Quality Ham-on-the-bone
from the Carvery   56p qtr.
NEW D-shaped Sliced Ham   35p qtr.
Bacon

1982 and the city gets set for a bumper Christmas with specially illuminated streets and activities.

Rain dampened the colourful spectacle of a pony parade through the city centre which was part of the Magical World of Christmas events. Children in fancy dress were lead in the parade by a coach bearing the Lord Mayor and Lady Mayoress and a sleigh carrying Father Christmas. However, crowds were happy to turn out with umbrellas in Market Street to see them.

A smile and a blessing from Pope John Paul II who arrives
for a historic visit to the North West in 1982.

Crowds turn out in their thousands at Heaton Park, to await the
arrival of the Pope, hoping he will see their messages.

To a rapturous welcome, the Pope tours Heaton Park, Manchester in his Leyland-built Pope-mobile greeting the people,
some of whom had camped overnight to see him in June 1982.

Commando chief in flying visit to fleet

THE chief of Britain's commando forces, Major-General Jeremy Moore, has paid a flying visit to the Falkland Islands fleet in the South Atlantic.

Gen. Moore conferred on *Fearless* (right) with Brig Julian Thompson, commander of the fleet's 3,000 assault troops, and Commodore Michael Clapp., the Navy's chief of amphibious warfare.

Fearless is the command ship from which the main body of troops could be flung at the beaches if Britain tries to retake the Falklands.

Argentine cuts mail link with Britain

ARGENTINA today cut off mail and telegraph communications with Britain, although telephone and Telex ties continued.

The government in Buenos Aires also said the joint chiefs would assume "control" over all foreign news published or broadcast in Argentina, but without direct censorship.

The directives were not totally clear, and the government told media executives: "If you have any doubt, consult the joint chiefs."

Only official communiques from the nation's ruling junta were considered reliable news about the conflict zone.

Although Argentina's million people are reported to be almost unanimous behind the recapture of the Falklands, and have reported the government's enthusiastic mass participation, an isolated few are beginning to question whether a war would be worth the price.

"We don't have money to spend on adventures like this," said a retired merchant seaman. "Argentina has plenty of land on this continent."

Radio broadcasts, probably produced by authorities but not specially identified, are warning Argentines not to commit "seditious acts."

FLASHPOINT!

Time's up—but still trying

By A SPECIAL CORRESPONDENT

THE FALKLANDS crisis is now at flashpoint. Forces of both sides are poised to attack unless diplomacy pays off at the last minute.

A total British blockade went into force at noon. Any planes and ships which come within 200 miles of the Argentine-occupied islands will be liable to attack by the powerful task force now assembled in the area.

And Britain has made it plain that this is no bluff.

The Buenos Aires decision to establish its own 200-mile "no-go" zone around the Falklands, as well as South Georgia, the Sandwich Islands and the Argentine mainland, means that bloody conflict could be only hours away.

Any British ship or plane found inside the zone would be regarded as hostile and "treated accordingly," said the three-man ruling junta.

The zone would operate "as of today" — apparently meaning immediately.

Meanwhile, the desperate peace efforts by America and the United Nations continue without pause.

Bishop calls for peaceful solution

THE Bishop of Manchester today called for a peaceful settlement in the South Atlantic as the Falklands crisis appeared to be close to a violent climax.

"I don't believe an armed invasion would achieve our two objectives of upholding the rule of law and safeguarding the lives, freedom and property of the islanders," he said.

"There could be untold dangers in such an invasion when the devastating power of modern weapons and the facts of distance are taken into account.

"Every possible pressure should be brought on the British Government in time to use means other than military to ensure that Argentine aggression is ended and a satisfactory long-term solution worked out.

DIVIDED

"If this would involve loss of face for our Government and country, it won't be better than the loss of many lives in the grim conditions of the South Atlantic.

"Efforts to secure the support of the United Nations have not yet been pursued to the limit. A UN peace-keeping force on the islands would be a better temporary solution than the efforts to reimpose British sovereignty by force.

"Christians are always divided over the use of armed force but those who are not pacifists can only back such methods when the foreseeable results would not offend justice and humanity more than the situation in which we find ourselves now. This cannot be so in the Falklands."

Although Argentina has been told Washington that its latest proposals are "unsatisfactory" and require further clarification, US Vice-President George Bush today said that Secretary of State Alexander Haig is "going the extra mile" to find a diplomatic solution.

And this afternoon Argentina's foreign minister Costa Mendez was due to meet United Nations Secretary General Javier Perez de Cuellar.

Diplomatic sources said the UN has "contingency plans" to act as intermediary and place an international "presence" on the islands, which Argentina occupied four weeks ago after 149 years of British rule.

But there were no indications so far of an understanding under which both Britain and Argentina would accept a peace-making role by the UN.

Mr Costa Mendez was expected to discuss all possible options. These include the appointment of a UN administrator or caretaker with a small administrative group which would be placed on the islands pending a diplomatic settlement.

Support

Washington administration sources said the United States might issue a statement in support of Britain if the crisis erupts into a military conflict.

And Vice-President Bush said: "I reiterate our fundamental support and the fundamental importance we place on our relationship with the United Kingdom, but I cannot comment further as long as we're trying to play a useful role."

It might also allow negotiations to restart, possibly through the United Nations, without giving the impression that Argentina had been humiliated by Britain.

But the critical question was whether Argentina would attempt to supply its troops on the Falklands after Britain's noon deadline.

Rumours in Buenos Aires that the junta might seek a pre-emptive strike against the task force were believed to be an attempt to keep Britain guessing.

It was accepted that Argentina had embarked on a high-risk strategy. If its aircraft carrier was sunk its whole fleet would be seriously damaged.

There was nothing in the latest Argentine communique to indicate what military action it would take against the British task force.

When a foreign reporter asked retired Admiral Jorge Fraga at a Press conference if the Argentine navy was at a disadvantage because it has British-made ships and missiles familiar to the enemy, he said: "No. For the same reason we are familiar with what they have."

At Westminster it is felt that Mrs Thatcher and her advisers will now have to calculate how far British public opinion will continue to support the Government if there are casualties in any numbers.

Many MPs feel that both sides are now engaged in a war of nerves.

Even if neither side seeks to provoke a conflict, accidental clashes could escalate the crisis.

The War Cabinet was examining the latest Argentine pronouncements to see if the door has been shut on further negotiations.

Some MPs feel the best hope lies with the United Nations, possibly by a direct intervention by the Secretary General, who is a Peruvian.

But Argentina's claim to sovereignty over the Falklands and Downing Street's commitment to self-determination for the islanders were still being seen as the crucial obstacle.

Clive to the rescue

Fireman Clive Moss rescued a drowning pub man from the River Douglas at Wallgate, Wigan.

He said by its condition it looked like it had spent...

Morale

COSTA MENDEZ
Meeting at UN

PEREZ DE CUELLAR
Peace in his hands?

Fleet's ice-cool hero: Page 17

Test tube twins are doing fine

BRITAIN'S first test tube twins, Daniel and Christopher Smith, were pronounced "healthy" today as they lay in their incubators.

They were born six weeks ahead of their scheduled NHS delivery at London's Royal Free Hospital.

Daniel, from Addiscombe Road, East Stockport, was delivered at twenty-five minutes past midnight yesterday in labour lasting 17 minutes.

"I think that the lad already breast-fed her babies, and is delighted," said Mr Harry Oxbridge.

The twins, born within 10 minutes, just before midnight, are the first test tube babies delivered on the NHS, he said.

Daniel weighed 4lb 16oz and Christopher 5lb 3oz.

The twins are being monitored in the hospital's special baby care unit. "They are not in danger, nor are they wired up," said Mr Oxbridge.

"They are both in a healthy state," he added. "The mother is very well and very happy."

Mrs Smith, and performer will have to stay in hospital more than a fortnight ago.

"We waited to have had by a couple of months in advance of the births," explained Mr Oxbridge.

"It is not unusual for twins to be born prematurely."

There had been no special problems during the deliveries supervised by Prof Ian Craft without any call for a Cesarian section.

The twins' father, Mr Stuart Smith, a postman, was in the middle of his daily round when the news was broken to him that his own very special delivery was on the way.

His boss, and postmaster Mr Derek Rawlinson, said Stuart's immediate reaction was: "Oh my God, it's happening."

Mr Rawlinson said: "The twins weren't due until early in June. Yesterday Stuart was out on a van run when the phone went.

"I took the call from a lady in the hospital's medical team. She sounded absolutely desperate and said Stuart must be told as soon as possible that his wife was going into labour. I left a message for Stuart because I thought I might have to go out of the office, but he returned while I was still there. He was going frantic. He had no money with him, so we gave him some cash to get him on his way and he was off like a shot.

"Ah! he could say was 'Oh my God'.

Stuart has worked from the Poynton office for about three years since he was transferred from Stockport.

Mr Rawlinson added:

"He's a tremendous lad. This couldn't have happened to a nicer couple. We are all tremendously delighted for Stuart and Jo, and people on his round will be equally happy for him."

Stuart's mother, who lives in Dumber Close, Poynton, declined to say anything.

The test-tube birth technique involves fertilising the female egg outside the mother and then implanting it in her womb.

Britain mastered the art first when Mr Patrick Steptoe and Dr Robert Edwards helped produce the world's first test tube baby, Louise Brown, who was born at Oldham in the summer of 1978.

And talking of twins ...

Perishers locked in a tight spot

EVERYONE but the Army was called in to help when the terrible Bowner twins struck again—and imprisoned themselves for nearly two hours.

By DAVID THOMAS

The panic started after haulage firm boss Stuart Bowner left the 23-month-old twins in his £15,000 American sports car while talking to a friend at the roadside.

Youngsters Stuart and James leapt into the front seat and CLUNK pressed the automatic door locking button — with the only set of keys still in the ignition.

BRRMM, BRRMM, they went, pretending to drive the 150 mph Corvette Stingray as dad puzzled how to get them out. Soon the horn was sounding and radio blaring as they fiddled with every switch in sight.

A large crowd gathered in New Street, Milnrow, near Rochdale, offering ideas. All the windows were firmly shut. It was impossible to smash them for fear of hurting the children and the windscreen could not be removed because it is sealed.

More people gathered round, the police were called and then the fire brigade. Friends and relatives tried to coax the children to unlock the doors without success.

Meanwhile, they were happily tucking into a tube of indigestion tablets, which meant drastic action was necessary. But freedom came just as firemen were about to closed through the car roof.

Mr Bowner borrowed a screwdriver to force a narrow gap above the door window. James pulled the keys from the ignition and passed them through.

Mr Bowner said: "A duplicate key would have been the answer, but they are impossible to obtain. I have tried before."

At home in Newhey Road, Newhey, near Rochdale, Mrs Jennifer Bowner, aged 31, told of the twins' previous escapades. James pushed a chair through a glass door and smashed a window with his head.

Baby Stuart had a paddle after emptying chip pan oil over the kitchen floor, he put toy cars in the washer and stuffed sweet papers in the cassette player.

And both just love cleaning the windows with jam butties.

Mrs Bowner said: "We never know what they'll do next — they are terrors. But they are just typical boys — and we love them."

Villa fined—but final spot safe

By PAUL HINCE

ASTON VILLA'S European Cup final place is safe — but the crowd riots which marred their semi-final against Anderlecht will cost £14,500 in UEFA fines.

Relieved Villa officials were informed early today that Anderlecht's protest had been rejected by a specially convened UEFA Commission which met in Zurich yesterday.

Anderlecht claimed their invasion of the pitch in the semi-final second leg to be replayed.

In imposing such a heavy fine, UEFA are clearly saying that Villa are responsible for their fans but did not think the incident serious enough to prevent the Midlands outfit facing Bayern Munich in the European Cup final on May 26.

However UEFA have also decided that Villa must play their next home European match behind closed doors. That game would take place next season providing Villa qualify for Europe by beating Bayern.

The UEFA Commission...

Raiders beaten off

Four masked raiders were beaten off by postmen when they attacked a sorting office in Manchester today.

The masked men, armed with coshes and pickaxe handles struck as a security van was being loaded up at the New Street sorting office in Miles Platting.

Only one of the postmen was slightly injured and the attackers fled when the bandit alarm was activated. Nothing was stolen.

STOP PRESS

Wounded paratrooper Ricky Westray received a rapturous welcome when he returned home to Chadwick Road, Middlewich, Cheshire ahead of his unit from the Falklands.

Marines Paul Griffin (left) and Russell Smith were in the first wave of troops to storm ashore in the battle of the Falkland Islands.

Paratrooper Paul Dale was pictured handing back the Union Flag to residents of Broughton House, the East Lancashire Home for disabled soldiers and sailors, in Salford. Paul's family had borrowed the flag to add a patriotic touch to his welcome home street party.

More street parties . . . and relatives, neighbours and friends greet John Davies, HMS Coventry survivor, as he arrives home.

Mark Anderson, a chef on the carrier HMS Hermes, was feted at a party in his honour when he returned from the Falklands.

Our Hero . . . Royal Marine Stephen Stoddard, serving with 42 Commando, gets a rousing welcome home from friends and relatives of Radnor Avenue, Denton, when he returns from the Falklands.

Neighbours turned out to greet returning Falklands Commando Chris Oakes, aged 19, of Shepherd Cross Street, Bolton, with a street party. Chris, based at Seaton in Plymouth, returned home on Canberra.

A FRIEND DROPPING IN   LATE CITY

Manchester Evening News

36,140   BRITAIN'S BIGGEST REGIONAL NEWSPAPER   THURSDAY, AUGUST 22, 1985   17p

Ringway jet fireball: 54 die

PATHWAY TO DOOM — *black smoke billows from the stricken jet in this dramatic picture taken by a Manchester Evening News reader from the scene at Ringway.*

TRAGIC END of holiday flight KT 328. Firemen battle to put out the flames

FIFTY - FOUR people were killed in a minute of horror today when a holiday jet burst into flames at Manchester Airport.

There were 83 survivors.

An explosion in the four-year-old Boeing's 737's port engine severed the aircraft's fuel lines and saturated it in fuel. Within seconds the aircraft had burst into flames.

Two stewardesses were thought to be among the dead.

The Civil Aviation Authority said this afternoon that it could not rule out the possibility of its demanding safety checks of all Boeing 737s held by airlines in this country.

The British Airtours Boeing bound for Corfu with 137 people aboard, caught fire as it was about to take off.

There were 129 passengers and two babies with six crew members.

A police spokesman said: "The whole tragedy took place within a minute."

The pilot had radioed air traffic control saying he was having difficulty with the engine.

The majority of the dead were sitting in the rear section of the aircraft. The heat from the fire on the wing was so powerful it burned through the fuselage.

More disaster news and pictures. Pages 2, 3, 4, 5, 30 and 31.

INSIDE — *Weather 2; Diary 6; Postbag 8; Lucky Addresses 12; BMDs 16; Business 17-18; Cartoons 34; Sport 56-60* **TV** 32-33.

The headlines say it all — and the picture sent in by a reader speaks volumes.

On the opposite page, the Prime Minister, Margaret Thatcher visits the scene of the crash.

From the left — Debbie Wilson, Harry Wardle, Claire Bailey, Mike Mather, Marke Tatlock and Alison Hughes are six of the survivors of the Manchester air disaster of September '85. Many people died after inhaling smoke when fire broke out on the Boeing 737. The six youngsters who had been out collecting money for the disaster fund handed over a cheque for £148 to John Bentley of the National Westminster Bank.

Seventy firemen tackled a blazing mill in Lower Broughton. It took four hours to bring the fire under control in March 1982.

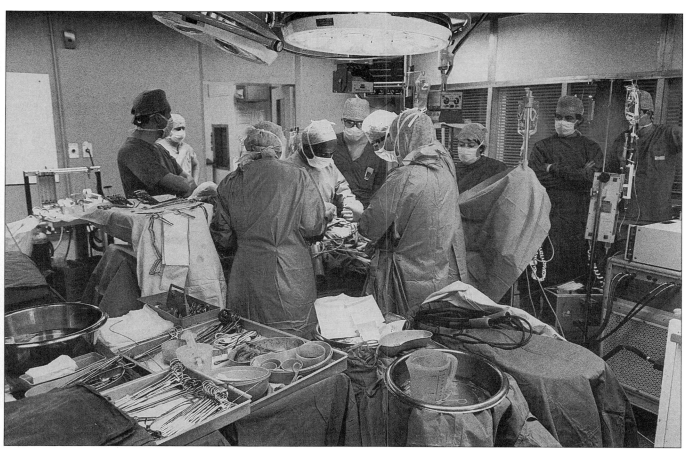

Evening News photographer John Fox and reporter Peter Harris were allowed to scrub up, don gowns and watch the first heart transplant at Wythenshawe hospital. At 4 15 am on April 11, 1987, a team of 20 led by Mr Ali Rahman, Consultant Cardio-Thorasic Surgeon at Wythenshawe Hospital, gently placed the new heart into the patient.

July 26, 1978 and gynaecologist Mr Patrick Steptoe (nearest the camera) and scientist Dr Robert Edwards talk to the world's press after the birth of the first test tube baby by caesarean section at Oldham General Hospital. The birth followed 12 years of research by Dr Edwards and his team at Cambridge University in consultation with Dr Steptoe at Oldham.

A boat sails on calm water in front of the spectacular Salford Quays backdrop.

Another impressive view of Harbour City at Salford Quays for the annualUniversity men's eights boat race, Manchester v Salford.

Moving in to the Museum of Science and Industry is one of Dr Who's nasties, a Cyberman. On the right two jugglers on unicycles perform during Castlefield Carnival, part of the Arts and Television Festival, which attracts thousands of visitors to the city in September.

A party of children arriving for an enjoyable day at this Lower Byrom Street warehouse, which forms part of the Manchester Museum of Science and Industry.

Going for Gold

Visionary of the nineties Bob Scott (on the right) and Rick Parry of Ernst & Young, later to become Chief Executive of the Premier League, survey the land at Dumplington, which was to be the site of one of the Olympic stadiums in March 1990. Bob first had the idea of bringing the Olympic Games to Manchester way back in 1984 and his sheer persistence and drive took us into bidding for the games for 1996 and the year 2000. After a truly magnificent bid for Britain, which has done so much for the north west and put Manchester firmly back on the map where it belongs, the IOC committee decided on September 23, 1993 that the Games for the year 2000 should go to Sydney, Australia. Mancunians were shocked and saddened at the result, but firmly believe that our team and their supporters in Monaco were true winners that day.

Princess Anne, supporter of the Manchester Olympic Bid and IOC member for Britain, with the managing director of Bovis, Dennis Bate, inspect the proposed arena site at Victoria Station.

A lone angler fishes in the canal as the structure of Manchester's Olympic Velodrome rises in the background.

Geoff Thompson, with five world karate titles under his belt is now chairman of the North West Sports Aid Foundation, centred in Manchester, and is also a roving ambassador for the Olympic Bid.

Manchester's Central Station, the northern end of the former Midland line from London — as it was in its heyday . . .

. . . and its transformation to G-MEX, a gigantic exhibition, concert and sports centre. In 1987 the project was nearing completion and the lights are being tested here prior to the official opening in March.

Destruction. A fire suspected to have been started by children badly damaged the stand at Swinton Rugby League Club.

Construction. A giant crane places the skeletal roof to Terminal 2 at Manchester International Airport October 1990.

A view of the giant Shell plant at Carrington in May 1989. *Pictured by John Fox.*

The Prime Minister John Major visiting British Aerospace at Warton near Preston early in '93 covered his ears from the aircraft noise — or was it that he couldn't listen to more crticism.
Photographer — Mike Grimes.

December 23, 1992. In another picture by Mike Grimes, the Lord Mayor of Manchester (right), the Lord Mayor of Trafford (left) and the Lord Mayor of Salford lay flowers on the high altar of Manchester Cathedral. The fifty candles mark the fifty years since the bombing during World War II. The Dean of the Cathedral, the Very Rev Robert Waddington, supervised the Commemorative Service.

A Prince for all seasons

'Are you wet...'? Prince Charles asked MEN photographer Eric Graham as he inspected the Cheshire Regiment during a downpour in Chester. Eric and his camera were in fact so wet that the camera lens had to be thrown away after this photographic session.

Prince Charles poses for our cameraman, John Fowler at Ordsall Library where he was meeting Prince's Trust grant recipients and residents of Ordsall estate. Lynn May our MEN journalist (in the check jacket) was a private guest of the Trust and afterwards wrote an exclusive feature about the visit and Prince Charles's work to help young people.

Manchester Evening News

FRIDAY MAY 8 1992   LATE CITY   30p

PAGE ONE COMMENT

Don't let Laura die

■ WAITING for a new life, little Laura Davies, four, smiles through her anguish. The operation she desperately needs is not available in Britain on the NHS and time is running out. Picture: JOHN FOWLER

Dear Mrs Bottomley,

Laura Davies is four years old. Her greatest wish is to be able to start school in September with her playmates.

But her wish may never come true. Laura is dying.

She was born with a rare bowel disorder, developed liver failure and has got only months to live.

You have the power to help save her life.

Generous

The double liver and bowel transplant operation she desperately needs is not yet available in Britain on the National Health Service but is being done successfully in America and doctors there are willing to operate on Laura.

But the surgery and after-care will cost a staggering £350,000. The generous

An open letter to new Health Secretary Virginia Bottomley

people of Greater Manchester have taken Laura, from Eccles, to their hearts and raised a magnificent £47,000 in just a few short weeks. Given time they would raise the rest.

But Laura Davies doesn't have that time.

Doctors say her small body is failing fast. The operation is her only hope. She cannot wait a decade for the same techniques to be developed here, cannot wait

for Britain to catch up, cannot wait for the NHS. She needs to go to America and she needs to go NOW.

Your health department says it is against the law for patients to be treated outside Britain on the NHS.

But rules can be changed. Alternatives can be found.

Your Government could and should give her the money. No one in the country would begrudge this little girl a

penny. Mercifully most illnesses can be treated in Britain, but Laura is a rare case. Her parents know that if they had the money their daughter could be saved.

Imagine their anguish as time runs out. They are being denied the basic right of treatment for their daughter because that treatment does not exist in this country.

Defied

For all her short life Laura has been fed through an intravenous drip. She has never had a birthday cake, never tasted ice cream.

You cannot sit back and deny her the chance of a normal life, you cannot sit back and watch her die. Laura has defied the odds already — she has re-written the rules.

Now it is your turn.

Sue them, says US hospital: Page 3

Charity begins at home

IF there is ever any doubt about the generosity and warm-heartedness of people in the north west, you only have to see the way they respond to an appeal for help, especially if that appeal is for a child. Little Laura Davies of Eccles captured all our hearts in 1992.

Born with a rare bowel disorder, at four years old she needed a double liver and bowel transplant to save her life. The 'News' led the way — and our readers responded by collecting a massive £200,000 to send Laura to America for treatment. The story became national news and King Fahd of Saudi Arabia, in an amazingly generous gesture, gave the remaining £150,000 needed.

Laura eventually required further operations to replace vital organs and the moral issues were debated around the world.

Another indefatigable fundraiser for Pendlebury Children's Hospital is Bryan Robson of Manchester United. The MUFC captain set out to raise £1.5 million for a new scanner for the hospital. Here he tries his hand at making a pizza at the Domino Pizza shop in Swinton before taking a batch along for the patients at the hospital.

In April 1992 above, Laura is pictured in Wakefield Ward of The Royal Manchester Childrens' Hospital, Pendlebury with her friends — from the left, Staff Nurse Sue Buckley, Staff Nurse Veronica McHugh and Staff Nurse Joanne Whitnall. *Photographer — Eric Graham.*

Concorde, the beautifully designed supersonic aircraft rests at Manchester International Airport.
Photographed by Clive Cooksey, Deputy Picture Editor.

A plane at the point of take-off at Manchester International Airport.

Opposite: Trams return to Manchester. After thirty three years rails are again laid in Manchester's streets for this hi-tech tramway system.
Two Metrolink trams are seen passing each other at the junction of High Street and Market Street.

And back to the News . . .

TOM WAGHORN — Feature writer, former chief sub-editor remembers Cross Street and Tom Henry who was Editor from 1946-1968.

EDITOR Tom Henry loved to hire his staff in unusual circumstances. In the early sixties I was on a Scottish climbing holiday and received a telegram: "Phone immediately. Reverse charges — Henry."

Within seven days, not having even applied for a job and with three weeks' holiday unused, I was Postbag editor. Cross Street then had an extension, the Dilworth Building, which was reached by a covered-in bridge. I shared a room "down the Dilworth" with John Alldridge, our star writer, city councillor, occasional Coronation Street scriptwriter and producer for Withington Players.

The swinging sixties they might have been in London, but the Evening News in those days ran on brown ale, black type and hot lead. Tom Henry ran his paper like an ironmaster, growling commands at his middle-aged executives who in turn snapped at the young reporters and subs who yelled at the humble copy-boys who ran the reporters' stories, sheet by sheet, to the chief sub-editor.

The boys crouched at the messengers' desk, this platoon of teenage runners, in the gloomiest corner of the editorial floor, making thick black tea in chipped mugs and leaping like scalded cats when some harassed hack shouted "Boy!"

We still have these messengers even in 1993, girls as well as boys and we still tend to run on brown ale, but the hot lead has been replaced by modern computer typesetting.

I think Tom Henry would have approved!

On the stone! Overseers and sub editors look on anxiously as Tom Henry, on the right, makes a last check of the front page before going to press.

In the composing room a Linotype operator turns the words into lines of type.

In the machine room, a heavy metal page is fitted to the huge presses.

Editorial conference at Cross Street with, from left to right Duncan Measor, 'Mr Manchester' of the Diary page; Doug Emmett Assistant Editor; Jack Able Picture Editor; James Ross News Editor, now Executive Editor; Tom Henry, Editor and Bill Pepper, Assistant Editor.

Transporting the 'News'

Manchester Evening News Morris vans line up in Warren Street opposite the Old Thatched House pub.

A 1956 van carried a 'bushing' machine, which could add the latest Stop Press news and results to the papers. They were particularly useful for football matches — and the modern, distinctive yellow and black 'mobiles' are used in the same way today.

Two delivery vans in 1971 wait outside the old Stockport Branch Office on Shaw Heath.

This picture shows the classified room at Cross Street in the fifties. Small ads are the lifeblood of any evening newspaper and are an ideal marketplace for anything from children's bicycles to cars or houses and jobs.

The modernised classified section at Deansgate in 1976.

A photographer finds a good spot to cover the Whitsuntide Walk.

Feature writers, including Andrew Grimes in the centre, with copy takers in the foreground at Cross Street.

Sportsdesk at Cross Street in 1967. On the left of our picture is David Meek, Manchester United reporter, on his left is Neville Bolton, our current Sports Editor. On the right of the picture (opposite Neville) is Vernon Addison who was the Sports Editor of the day, and on his right is George Dowson who now covers Rugby League.

Goodbye Cross Street

The mammoth operation moving from Cross Street to Deansgate in August 1970 was a far-sighted idea to share the resources of one publishing plant at Northcliffe House on Deansgate. The new buildings adjacent held the editorial, advertising and commercial offices of The Guardian, Daily Mail, Sunday People and ourselves. No newspapers were in direct opposition and it meant that the presses were used night and day.

The top two pictures show the heavy Linotype machines being taken out and tied securely to a transporter for the short journey to Deansgate.

Hello Deansgate

Settled in its new home, the first Deansgate-printed copies of the Manchester Evening News were anxiously scanned by Ken Searle MEN Managing Director on the left, Andy Harvie, later Managing Director, who was in charge of the move, Hirst Adams from the firm of architects, Leach, Rhodes and Walker, and Max Dallas, from Associated Newspapers.

The whole move was made within 24 hours from the final edition of the Pink Sports paper being printed at Cross Street on Saturday, to the Guardian being printed at Deansgate on the Sunday evening so that no editions of either paper were lost.

BRIAN REDHEAD - Previously Northern Editor of the Guardian, Brian became Editor of the 'News' in 1969 and left in 1975. He is now the senior presenter of the BBC's 'Today' programme, but remains a great supporter of Manchester.

Brian Redhead the Editor in 1971 and Tom Henry, former Editor of the Manchester Evening News survey the new stainless steel statue of Vigilance in Spinningfield, designed by Keith Godwin head of the School of Sculpture, Manchester Polytechnic, Faculty of Art and Design.

DOUG EMMETT - From his position as Assistant Editor, Doug took over as Editor and supervised the change from broadsheet to a tabloid newspaper in 1983. He retired in November of that year but sadly died in July 1988.

Bob Corfield, photographer in the centre surrounded by his colleagues, is seen at his retirement presentation after 50 years at the Manchester Evening News.

On the right, is the last broadsheet issue of the Manchester Evening News published on Saturday March 12, together with the new tabloid shape which was published on the Monday. The slogan - much repeated at the time - 'A Friend Dropping In' was used in the announcement of the new paper .... that it was intended to be 'A Better Friend Than Ever'.

A FRIEND DROPPING IN

FINAL

Manchester Evening News

35,396   SATURDAY, MARCH 12, 1983   15p

FULL WEEKEND TV AND RADIO GUIDE INSIDE

BRITAIN'S BIGGEST REGIONAL EVENING NEWSPAPER

COMING ON MONDAY: A BETTER FRIEND THAN EVER

LOOK OUT on Monday for your new-look tabloid Friend. Modern, exciting, easier to read, your Friend will be better than ever in its crisper, brighter style with . .

● Page after page of local, national and international news.

● All your favourite features

● The best in sports coverage

● A complete Business World service

AND

● A new-look two-page TV and radio guide.

And there will be thousands of pounds to be won on Bingo and X-Ball.

We've got a new shape

AND NOW IT'S YOUR TURN TO

SHAPE UP

Are you fit to face up to the rigours of modern life? Well next week you can shape up with the News as we get the low-down on healthy living.

PLUS

A new strip to help you get fit, with easy - to - follow exercises to get you in shape.

Murder quiz man's collapse

A MAN detained for interview about a murder was today in hospital after an incident at a police station.

Police did not name him, but a spokesman said he had collapsed while being subdued during an incident at Coventry headquarters late last night.

Officers from the Metropolitan Police were waiting to take the man to London for questioning in relation to a murder last November.

They went to the assistance of the Coventry officers and in a struggle, the spokesman added, it was noticed that the man was in difficulty with his breathing and was given the kiss of life.

Today he was in an intensive care unit with relatives at his bedside.

Grenade attack

A man was slightly injured in a grenade attack on a West Belfast police station today.

Two grenades were thrown over the fence at the rear of the Springfield Road military base, exploding in the yard.

A man who had called to speak with police, is understood to have received a shrapnel wound to a hand. An unexploded grenade was found outside.

Sports clinic opened by MP

A health centre for the treatment of injured sportsmen, and to cater for people wishing to tone up, was officially opened by Macclesfield MP Mr Nicholas Winterton at Macclesfield Town FC's Moss Rose ground.

The Olympian Clinic is the brainchild of Dr John Whiteside, the soccer club's medical officer, and his wife Tricia.

AIRPORT FLAP

'Cop in hu... for lo... girl, 4

POLICE were ... today for fou... Marie Payne, who... while playing ... home yesterday af...

A helicopter ... were being used ... the area near De... Dagenham, East Lo...

"We only hope ... find her quickly ... there are so many... in the area that co... a young girl," said... spokesman.

Marshland, the ... riverbank and de... sites were being ... for fair-haired Marie...

Police believed ... seen at 5.45 last nig... ing towards Barking... A13 road...

They said crime w... suspected.

Backing f... Argentin...

Ending their summ... New Delhi today, the ... aligned states recognis... Falkland Islands, ... Georgia and South San... Islands as integral par... Latin America belongin... Argentina.

FIRST EXTRA

A BETTER FRIEND THAN EVER

Manchester Evening News

15p

MONDAY, MARCH 14, 1983

25,397

Ex-girlfriend at different court

ABOVE (left) Sue Stephens, the model appearing in court today; and shooting victim Pc Nick Carr, who was wounded in the groin.

THE NEW
Manchester Evening News
says
Hello
with

64 PAGES

This is an historic day for Manchester with the introduction of the new brighter, handier Manchester Evening News tabloid. We have had many congratulations sent to us and we thank all those who have wished us well, including, of course, advertisers and newsagents.

GUIDE TO THE NEW PAPER

TV and Radio Guide — Pages 32 and 33
Weather — Page 2
Local, national and international news — 2, 3, 4, 5, 7, 9, 13, 17, 19, 20, 45
Mr Manchester — Page 6
House Price Shock — Page 10
Shape-up with the News — Pages 14 & 15
Music and the Arts — Page 16
Meet Hayley Mills — Page 16
Your views in our Postbag — Page 18
Street of Success — Page 21
It's Entertainment — Page 31
Horoscope, crossword and cartoons — Page 44
Business World — Pages 53, 54 and 55
Sport — Pages 58-64
Classified guide — Page 22

X-BALL
PAGE 58

RING OF STEEL FOR MARTIN

By FRED HACKWORTH

MAXIMUM security surrounded David Martin today when he appeared in court to be sent for triad on 14 charges.

He was brought to London's Lambeth court in a police van with an escort of officers in cars at both front and rear.

The court itself had been turned into a virtual fortress. Higher walls had been built in the courtyard, along with a barrier of metal spikes.

It was believed many of the officers guarding 35-year-old Martin within the court's ring of steel were armed.

Martin, of Crawford Place, Marylebone, is accused of attempting to murder Pc Nick Carr, aged 36, who was shot in the groin at a video-tape warehouse last August.

The other charges against Martin relate to four alleged firearms offences; four burglaries; two thefts; one robbery; and two dishonest handlings.

The tiny court was packed as Martin was brought before the chief local magistrate, Mr Maurice Guymer.

Meanwhile, several miles away at Marylebone court, Martin's former girlfriend, Sue Stephens, was appearing with two other men.

Stephens, a 25-year-old model, of Hampstead, and film editor Lester Purdy, 29, of Palmers Green, are accused of assisting in the removal and retention of stolen property on behalf of Martin.

Peter Exter, aged 25, an electrician, of Notting Hill, is charged with handling the property.

(Proceeding)

DAVID MARTIN . . . he faces 14 charges.

£16,000 haul

Cassettes worth £16,125 were stolen from a warehouse in Tilson Road, Baguley, Manchester.

£78,000 will

Saul Goldstone, of Macavin Avenue, Chorltoncum-Hardy, Manchester, who died in May, left £78,257 gross (£73,492 net).

Marathon goes on for jury

LATE FLASH: Judge said he would accept majority verdict.

By DON FRAME

THE JURY in the nine-week-long police conspiracy trial at Manchester Crown Court were back behind locked doors again today after spending their fourth night in an hotel.

The seven women and five men have so far spent almost 22 hours trying to reach a verdict on four detectives and a housewife accused of conspiring to pervert the course of justice.

Their retirement, which began at lunchtime last Thursday, is already one of the longest on record.

Mr Justice Caulfield had to apply to the Lord Chancellor for permission for a rare Sunday sitting of the court yesterday.

The jury, looking weary after their fourth day of deliberations, made only a two-minute appearance in court to be formally dismissed until they reconvened today.

Before the court are Detective Constable David Kirwin, aged 28, of Westwood Road, Heald Green; Dc John Ellis, aged 30, of Radnormere Dr, Cheadle Hulme; Dc John Holmes, aged 35, of Longhope, Forest of Dean, Gloucestershire; Det-Sgt Royston Smith, aged 40, of Poise Brook Road, Offerton, Stockport; and Mrs Ethel

Parkes, aged 41, of Caldervale Avenue, Chorlton.

All plead not guilty to the conspiracy charge. Dc John Ellis alone also pleads not guilty to a charge of corruption alleging acceptance of a £100 bribe.

Left turn

Left - winger Jimmy Knapp looks set to emerge this week as the new leader of the National Union of Railwaymen. His federation with the train drivers' union.

BL strike called off

THE strike at British Leyland's car body plant in Cowley, Oxford, was called off by 2,000 workers today. But a union official warned there could be more trouble if the company persisted with its "bullying tactics."

At BL's other main plant, Longbridge, in Birmingham, 200 storemen were deciding whether to continue a stoppage which halted production of three models after police raids on some of the men's homes.

Production at Cowley was hit twice last week, disrupting the Rover, Acclaim and Ambassador body lines.

The men objected to new levels, but manning returned to work after a formula was agreed between union officials and the company.

But there was a further walk out of 170 paint shop men towards the end of the week, and workers met today to decide whether to support them.

(Earlier story: Page 57)

An inspector who went to ...

A man was later charged with endangering the lives of train passengers.

SEE PAGE 16

The days of our Manchester Evening News Ladies Golf Competition and the Editor, Doug Emmett is seen here at a presentation dinner with some of our glamorous lady golfers and their trophies.

At the 'News' Search for a Star contest in 1981 the winner was a young lady from Rochdale — 14 year old Lisa Stansfield.

We had some great children's parties at the Circus when it came to Belle Vue. The children here meet the clowns before the performance.

he Manchester Evening News Theatre Dance Festival was held every year in July. Its home for many years was the Exhibition Hall at he top of Lewis's department store. Children from dancing schools all over the north west competed and the presentation ceremony was lengthy as there were trophies for each of the many different sections.

'Variety Show for the Elderly' is held each year at the Free Trade Hall and organised by Dave Eager and his friends from the tertainment world. Visiting celebrities such as Eartha Kitt, Emile Ford, Karl Denver and Stuart Hall have entertained our delighted senior citizens.

The 'News' organised literary lunches in Manchester from 1986 in various venues around the city. In the top picture, left to right, are Eleanor Bron, Sheridan Morley and Lady Antonia Fraser. Immediately above, from left to right, are Jean Metcalf with her husband, Cliff Michelmore, and Pamela Tudor-Craig.

In 1992, a Newspapers in Education initiative was started by the Editor's secretary, Janis Pearson, who now looks after this important section full time. A special newspaper 'Heartbeat of a Great City' was printed and a video 'Life in the Fast Lane' produced as an introduction to her talks to school children.

The Manchester Evening News is renowned as the paper which pays for itself and samplings, discount offers and free-to-enter competitions appear regularly. The armchair gamblers among our readers pay a modest amount to enter our Spot-the-Ball competition. A phenomenal jackpot of £81,500 was won in March 1993 by Miss Tracy Cully, of Didsbury, who was presented with her cheque by Norman Rossington.

Where would we be without our news agents and newsboys! Paperboy Adam Tildsley defied the agony of a broken wrist to finish his round after falling off his bike in November 1992. The 13-year-old from Romiley, Stockport was soon back on his rounds, but on foot and with a plaster cast on his arm.

Capital of entertainment

Manchester has a great tradition in music — from the Hallé Orchestra to pop groups such as Simply Red. Live musical entertainment for everyone! There are also musical schools such as Chethams.

Chetham's hospital school was founded by Humphry Chetham, a Manchester Grammar School boy, who became a manufacturer of woollen cloth and a moneylender, amassing a great fortune. He became very prominent and in 1648 opened negotiations to establish a school in Manchester for the education and maintenance of forty 'poor boys'. It is now one of the greatest specialist music schools in the world. The original building is still intact, but additional buildings have been added to house the growing number of pupils. The students below celebrate Founders Day in 1957 and dress appropriately for a service at Manchester Cathedral.

The Duchess of Kent stops to look at some instruments in the glass cases in the library of the Northern College of Music, Manchester, in June 1973, after the official opening. She is currently President of the college which is now the Royal Northern College of Music.

The Hallé Orchestra in concert at The Free Trade Hall. The Orchestra was formed by Sir Charles Hallé who also created the Royal Manchester College of Music. The orchestra, Britain's oldest professional orchestra, was formed in 1858.

The Manchester-based BBC Philharmonic is now one of Europe's finest orchestras. Guest conductor John Hopkins, on the right, rehearses the orchestra in 1989. He was formerly the principal conductor with the orchestra in the fifties. With him is Trevor Green, Head of Music, BBC North.

1983 and the Hallé's brass and percussion section play the Fanfare for the Common Man on the steps of the Town Hall, Manchester, to announce their 125th birthday appeal.

Popular music of the sixties and Manchester played its part; the first Top of the Pops was broadcast on New Year's day, 1964, from a converted church in Dickenson Road, Rusholme. Around this time, Harpurhey lad Freddie Garrity formed Freddie and the Dreamers, seen here at rehearsal.

Another local group Herman's Hermits was formed in 1963.

1966 — Eric Haydock, top guitarist with the Manchester-based group The Hollies, pictured with his wife.

A 1993 picture of Derek Leckenby, of Herman's Hermits, with student Phil Holden before Derek and Barry Whitman joined North Area College, Heaton Moor, Stockport in a fund-raising concert.

The nineties and Steven Morrisey appears at the Apollo, Manchester.

Another Manchester group, Happy Mondays, at a Cities in the Park concert in 1991.

Lowry and his art

A well known figure in Manchester until his death in February 1976, Laurence Stephen Lowry, was a gentle, unassuming man who was surprised by his fame. Born in Manchester in 1887, this painter concentrated largely on transferring to canvas his impressions of the city and its surroundings. His 'matchstick figures' set against backgrounds of factories and football grounds are unmistakable although many have tried to copy this style.

Photograph by Maurice Hatton of Camera Press, London.

Greater Manchester is rich in public and private art galleries. Visitors are attracted to them not only for the wonderful paintings, but for events such as this auction at Manchester City Art Gallery in 1991.

Students from South Manchester College with their window display at Manchester Museum for the Festival of Expressionism in 1992

Dr Rosalie David keeper of Egyptology at Manchester Museum pictured in 1989. The museum has one of the leading collections of Egyptology and Dr David has headed the research team since 1972.

March 1983 and two year old Benjamin Green is dwarfed by the Avro Shackleton aircraft which dominates the aircraft museum in Liverpool Road, Manchester. Benjamin was getting a sneak preview of the museum before the official opening. The Air and Space Museum is part of the Castlefield Urban Heritage Park.

Show Time

The theatre in Greater Manchester is second to none, Bolton, Oldham, Tameside all have thriving theatres and Manchester can boast of the Palace Theatre (above) and the Opera House for the big scale ballet and operatic productions, plus such superb musicals as Les Misérables and 42nd Street. The chorus for which lines up on stage on the right. The city also has the Contact and Library theatres, The Green Room and Nia Centre.

Warren Clarke (left) who plays Bosco and Paul Chapman as Harwell Mincing get ready for the shooting of Granada's Christmas show in 1986 The Antelope Christmas. Warren was a messenger boy at the Manchester Evening News who was always mimicking people and finally decided to go in to acting.

A celebrity knees-up by stars who have appeared at the BBC Play-house theatre in Hulme where many took their first steps to stardom. From left to right, Harry Worth, Cardew Robinson, Bill Waddington, The Beverley Sisters and Tom Mennard.

Right — Sylvia Syms and Dora Bryan enjoy a chat and a glass of wine.

The old Cotton Exchange in Manchester lives again with a modern theatre-in-the- round. Its ultra modern exterior and superb facilities attracts top actors and actresses, writers and directors. Here, first-nighters gather for the opening night in September 1976.

MANCHESTER EVENING NEWS THEATRE AWARDS are now in their twelfth year and they recognise the importance of theatre in Greater Manchester. A few famous faces from award ceremonies during the twelve years are featured here. On the right is Nicholas Parsons, who has compered the ceremony so brilliantly and professionally for the last five years, and will do so again in November 1993. With him is veteran actress Joan Turner. Below right is Salford born Robert Powell with two prizewinners. Below on the left is Louis Emmerick, Eammon O'Neal and Becky Want and immediately below is Liam Neesom, now a Hollywood actor.

As a final accolade to the importance of theatre in the region, Manchester has been chosen as City of Drama 1994.

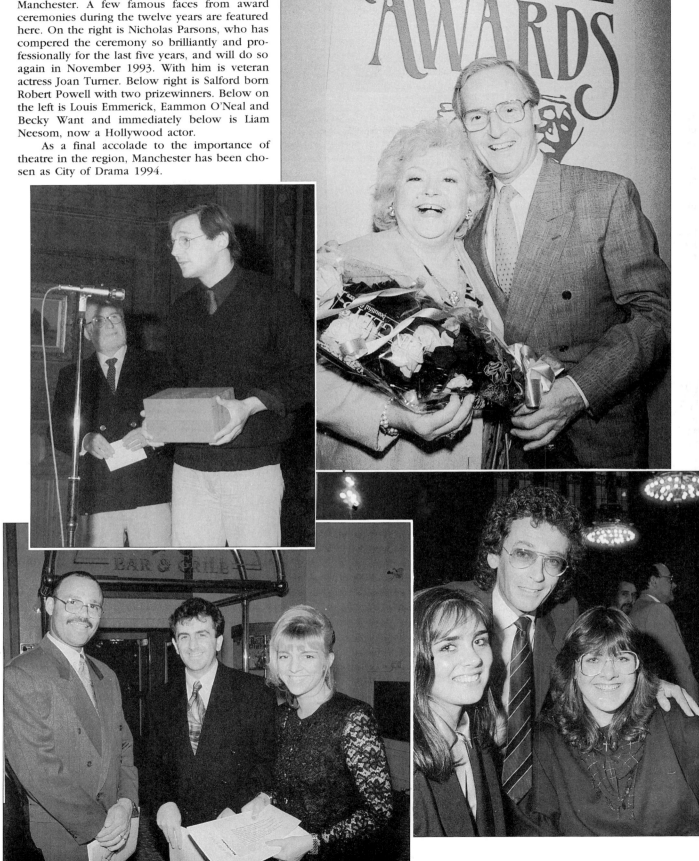

Sporting Heroes

NEVILLE BOLTON — Sports Editor of the Manchester Evening News.

Sport is the heartbeat of the North West region and the Manchester Evening News has always been the taker of that mighty pulse.

Old Trafford football and cricket grounds and Maine Road have all been the stages for some of the greatest events in sport and homes to a host of undying legends.

There was the tragedy of the Munich Air disaster in which eight of the famous Manchester United Busby Babes lost their lives; the glory of United's 1968 European Cup triumph and this year's FA Carling Premiership Trophy. Manchester City, have had their magic moments, too, they won the Division One title in 1968, the FA Cup in 1969 and the League Cup and European Cup Winners Cup in 1970.

The area is packed with the best in almost every other major sport. Wigan remain 'simply the best' in Rugby League, the world's tennis stars play at Didsbury, world championship boxing is regularly staged at Manchester's G-Mex, and the superstars of golf are regular visitors to a region which has one of the greatest concentration of courses in the world.

Whatever the major — or minor — event and wherever the big news is happening, the Manchester Evening News and Pink sports teams, two of the most experienced and respected in the business, have always been right in the thick of the action.

The northern Rugby League clubs are hard to beat. Pictured here are Swinton, who have just won the 1963 League Championship.

Jackie Brown from Manchester is the British and Empire, European and World Flyweight Champion in 1932.

Johnny King, with his Lonsdale Belt, fought for the Bantam-weight world title in 1933.

King George V makes the first Royal visit to the provinces for a football match. The occasion was Manchester City v Liverpool on March 27, 1920 at City's ground, which was then in Bennett Street, off Hyde Road.

Jock McAvoy, British Middle and Light-weight Champion, who fought for the world title in 1936.

Peter Kane was World Flyweight Champion in 1938. Here he poses with Gracie Fields who presents him with his title belt.

Salford win the Rugby League Challenge Cup in 1938/39. Albert Gear, Salford, scores the winning try against Barrow at Wembley.

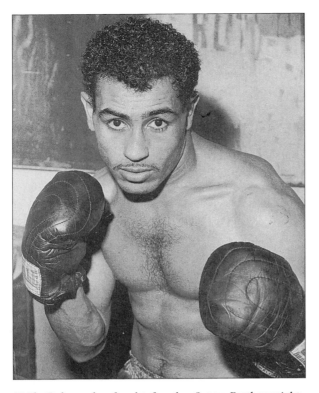

Najib Daho, who fought for the Super Featherweight world title in 1986, was tragically killed in a car crash in 1993.

Pat Barrett who fought for the world light welterweight title in 1991.

No, not Haydock Park Racecourse, where Lester Piggot rode his first winner in 1948, or Aintree, home of the Grand National. This was Manchester's own racecourse, Castle Irwell. The last race was run in 1963.

United become the first English team to win the European Cup in May 1968. Bobby Charlton — one of the original 'Busby Babes', survivor of the Munich crash and already a soccer legend — and Shay Brennan with the Cup aloft lead their victorious team round the Wembley ground.

British football's most controversial figure in 1971 and every boy's hero, George Best at a training session.

Before the European Cup match in 1968 a solemn Bobby Charlton leads his team on to the pitch. Behind Charlton are Alex Stepney, Brian Kidd, George Best with the ball at his feet, John Aston, Billy Foulkes (half hidden), Tony Dunn and David Sadler.

The 'Blues' let the world know about it! They have won the European Cup Winners Final at Vienna winning 2-1 against Gornik Zabrze. From the steps of the Town Hall, Manchester, in front of cheering fans, the ebullient Francis Lee takes over as cheer leader, joined by Malcolm Allison, holding the Cup and Mike Summerbee on the right with Tony Book behind.

Flashback to 1956 where we see the Manchester City 'Blues' returning to a civic reception at the Town Hall, Manchester after beating Birmingham 3-1 to win the FA Cup.

Weightlifting champion David Mercer of Tyldesley winner of a gold medal at the 1987 European Championships.

Reg Harris, of Bury, dominated sprint cycling in the post war years winning five world titles between 1947 and 1954. He also won two silver medals at the 1948 Olympics in London.

Brian Duncan, a local bowling champion from Bamber Bridge, who has won the Waterloo Handicap five times.

Manchester City Football Team, August 1973. The club hit the headlines in 1993 when the management was challenged and criticism came from supporters and previous players, including millionaire Francis Lee (bottom right).

Radcliffe's John Spencer won the world professional snooker championship in 1969, 1971 and 1977.

Peter Craven of Belle Vue Speedway pictured in 1963 with the World Individual Championship Trophy, the Golden Helmet Match Race Trophy and the Match Race Championship Trophy. He also won the championship in 1955.

Picture of an annual top football club photocall: Manchester United lining up in 1975.

Peter Collins is welcomed home by family and friends after winning the world individual speedway championship in 1976.

Martin Grimley, one of the 1987 England World Cup hockey squad.

Neil Fairbrother, a young Lancashire and England cricketer pictured in 1987.

Manchester hurdler Shirley Strong, aged 24, preparing in 1984 for the Los Angeles Olympics where she won a silver medal.

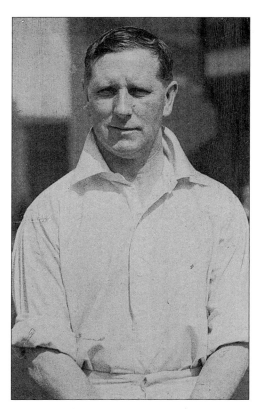

Ernest Tyldesley was a Lancashire County cricketer in the golden years of the twenties. His brothers Dick and James also played for the county.

Andrew Murray, who won the European Open Golf Championship in 1989

Close friends Diane Edwards and her Sale Harriers' team mate Ann Williams came first and second in the 800 metres final in the Commonwealth Games in Auckland in 1990 winning the gold and silver medals. At their joyful return to England they are greeted at Manchester Airport by 18 month old Nadine, niece of Di Edwards. Pictured from left to right are Paula Dunn another silver medal winner, Di Edwards, Nadine and Ann Williams.

Eric Evans is having a bit of fun with Manchester United centre forward Tommy Taylor at Old Trafford football ground in 1958. Evans captained England at Rugby Union 1948 to 1958.

Fran Cotton of Sale also captained The Lions during the years he played for England (1972 to 1981) — and provides the current team with their shirts!

Dewi Morris, Orrell and England scrum-half and his wife Penny are congratulated on their wedding by England and British Lions team mates - August 1993.

Another British Lions' captain, Tony Neary was at one time the most capped England player. He left the International scene with 46 caps.

Billy Beaumont, as captain of the England Rugby Union team, runs on to the field to the delight of the crowd in 1981. He is now more widely known for TV's 'A Question Of Sport'.

Rugby League and Swinton v Widnes in February 1992. Swinton's Joe Faimolo is halted by Widnes's Alan Tait and David Hulme.

Swinton Rugby League players celebrate in the traditional bath tub after winning a match 44-8 in 1975.

Wigan parade the Rugby League Trophy for their fans in 1987. In 1993 they win the Challenge Cup at Wembley for the sixth successive year, making them one of the greatest Rugby League teams of all time.

The Manchester Evening News Sports Personality of the Year for 1992 was super swimming star Sarah Bailey, aged 15 years. Sarah looking more like a model at the ceremony won two gold, three silver and two bronze at the 1992 Paralympics held in Barcelona. Sports Personalities of the Month David White of Manchester City on the left and Lee Sharpe of Manchester United on the right are pictured with Sarah after the ceremony at the Midland Hotel.

Enjoying a chat are Bob Scott, co-ordinator of Manchester's Olympic Games Committee; Robert Atkins, Minister for Sport and former Lancashire and West Indies captain Clive Lloyd at the 1991 Sports Personality Awards at the Ramada Renaissance Hotel. These popular sports awards are sponsored by Boddingtons - the 'Cream of Manchester.'

Hard news

PAUL HORROCKS — News Editor of the Manchester Evening News gives us an insight into the news gathering operation of a newspaper.

HARD NEWS . . . It's the lifeblood of newspapers, and one of the main reasons why most people buy the MEN.

We carry local, national, and international news, gathered by our own team of reporters and photographers, backed by correspondents all over the world. It's a fast and aggressive business, but never dull.

We reflect people's lives, their dreams and their tragedies.

Time is the enemy. With five editions per day, each requiring updated information as stories change or new ones break, deadlines have to be met. The paper won't wait.

News reporters rush out of court to file a story with minutes to spare before the next edition is completed. Often there's no time to even sketch an outline of the story — it's straight on to the telephone and dictate copy from shorthand notes. Complicated facts have to be marshalled into an easy to follow style.

Photographers must calculate just how much time to wait at the scene of a crime or at a football match, before leaving for the office to process their pictures. Fast moving technology means that sometimes pictures can be transmitted by phone line, and reports filed on lap top computers.

But where do all the different stories come from. The MEN newsroom puts in dozens of calls each day to the emergency services. Contacts built up over years are checked by our specialist writers. And the greatest source of information — our own readers — call the newsdesk to tell us something new. No two days are ever the same.

I spent 15 years as an on the road reporter, and saw things and met people I shall never forget.

When the Moors murder inquiry reopened at Saddleworth I was the paper's crime correspondent and spent hours in the pouring rain waiting for details of the police operation. Finally, when Myra Hindley was brought back to the scene of her crime, hundreds of journalists were despatched to the desolate moor, in driving snow,to watch a distant figure in overalls and red gloves helping police in their grisly search for bodies.

The twisting and turning of the Stalker affair, its political intrigue and police secrecy was fascinating.But the pressure to be first with the latest development was wearing.

I shall never forget a Wednesday night in Lockerbie, just before midnight, walking along dark, winding, lanes littered with the shattered fragments of a Pan-Am jumbo jet, wondering how such a huge aircraft could be smashed into so many tiny pieces. The smell of aircraft fuel was heavy in the air.

In Zeebrugge harbour I joined a mob of journalists, all pushing to be first on board a tug to circle the overturned hulk of the Herald of Free Enterprise ferry in which 188 had died. Making notes from the quayside was one thing, but to get so close to a half submerged ferry, lying on its side was an experience which silenced everyone of us watchers.

Now, as news editor I am indoors and the journalists file their reports to me to be checked and passed to the editor. I am continually looking forward, trying to forecast which way a story will turn. It's like a game of chess, ensuring your team are in the right place at the right time to gain the maximum information in the most professional way. It's a hard game.

Paul Horrocks (centre) at an interview given by search chief Peter Topping in 1987.

December, 1986 and after more than two decades, Myra Hindley returns to the scene of her horrific crime. She was helping police to trace the remaining graves on the desolate Saddleworth Moor.

A flashback to police on duty on the mist-covered moors near where the body of 10-year-old Lesley Downey was found in a shallow grave near the Greenfield to Holmfirth Road at Wessenden Head.

Manchester Evening News
and Chronicle

FRIDAY, MAY 6, 1966   30,018   PRICE 4d

Moors TODAY'S CLOSING SCENES AT THE ASSIZES **Trial**

MOORS TRIAL VERDICT

BOTH GUILTY: LIFE FOR BRADY, HINDLEY

'Calculated, cruel and cold-blooded'

BY STAFF REPORTERS
Chester, Friday.

AFTER a trial lasting 14 days, and after one of the most sensational murder cases ever investigated by police in the North, the Moors Trial jury at Chester Assizes reached their verdicts:

IAN BRADY, aged 28, stock clerk, of Wardle Brook Avenue, Hattersley, near Hyde, charged with murdering Edward Evans, Lesley Ann Downey, and John Kilbride.

He was found guilty of all three murders.

He was sentenced to life imprisonment concurrently on the three charges.

MYRA HINDLEY, aged 23, shorthand typist, of Wardle Brook Avenue, Hattersley, near Hyde, charged with murdering Edward Evans, Lesley Ann Downey, and John Kilbride, and also with harbouring Brady knowing he had murdered Kilbride.

She was found guilty of murdering Evans and Downey and not guilty of murdering Kilbride.

She was found guilty of being an accessory to Kilbride's murder.

She was sentenced to life imprisonment concurrently on two murder charges and to seven years' imprisonment concurrently on the accessory charge.

The judge told Brady : "These were three calculated, cruel, cold-blooded murders."

The judge continued to Brady : "In your case I pass the only sentence which the law now allows, which is three concurrent sentences of life imprisonment."

The judge also said : "In your case, Hindley, you have been found guilty of two equally horrible murders and in your case on the two murders I will pass concurrent sentence of life imprisonment and on the charge of being an accessory a sentence of seven years' imprisonment."

The jury had retired at 2.40 pm from the historic courtroom.

Mr Justice Fenton Atkinson had summed up to the all-male jury for five hours.

The jury returned first at 4.21 pm, but it was only to ask for legal advice about two revolvers said to belong to Hindley. They retired again and returned to give their verdict at 4.56.

● Background to Moors murders—Page 7.

These three people died

Lesley Downey   John Kilbride   Edward Evans

'Six' Brown puts British terms for entry

By a Special Correspondent

BRITISH Economic Minister Mr George Brown said in Stockholm today that Britain wants to be a member of an expanded Common Market and is seeking the basis on which this would be possible.

He was opening a debate on European affairs in a world context on the second day of the Socialist International Congress.

Mr Brown pledged that Britain would fulfil her responsibilities to Europe and play a full part in achieving European unity.

No hint

Mr Brown said that when Britain applied again for membership of the Common Market...

More showers

Keep your umbrella handy. Today's weather report from Manchester Weather Centre...

Judge: We can't forget tape

Chester, Friday.

MR JUSTICE FENTON ATKINSON, completing his summing-up at the Moors trial today, told the all-male jury : "Those of us who heard that Lesley Downey tape recording are not likely to forget for a very long time."

The accused, Ian Brady and ash-blonde Myra Hindley, listened as intently as the jury in a hushed and crowded courtroom...

Water from Lakes: Go-ahead to city

By Political Correspondent

MANCHESTER is to be allowed to take from Windermere water—but with...

Loan plea

Water level

● Turn to Page 16

Cost could top £30,000

NOW it is over. And how much has the Moors Trial cost? Experts today estimated a figure in the region of £30,000.

Tapes to go into 'Black Museum'?

HARROWING tape recordings played in the Moors Trial will, together with other exhibits, form exhibits in the case...

Pay rise for lorrymen

Now CID chief can hunt fish

BY A STAFF REPORTER

'Life' means just that

WHAT is a life sentence?

A "life" sentence is exactly that. A prisoner may be released if the parole board...

Windows are smashed

ONCE again crowds gathered outside the windows and doorways...

● Ian Brady and Myra Hindley. Special pictures issued today by the police.

This shocking picture was taken by our photographer Eric Graham, unknown to the man who was threatening to strangle a woman hostage during a siege at a flat in Levenshulme. All press had been banned from the area. The woman was later released and the man arrested. The exclusive picture was used on the MEN front page and also in the national papers the following day. It was also useful to police as an aid to convicting the man of the crime.

Big cities all have their problems and unrest in Moss Side erupted in riot scenes in 1981. Shops were set alight and this dramatic picture was taken by Clive Cooksey.

Who would choose to be a policeman! Youths, one of them masked, menace police who are sheltering behind their riot shields. Some of the youths taunted the officers and, from the rear of this crowd, bricks were thrown.

The reporting of such occasions in a fair, unbiased and accurate way is important. It is big news. People want — and need to know the facts. When a big news story breaks, the reporters and photographers get to the centre of the action.

The Stalker Affair

There was much support in Manchester for John Stalker following his suspension from office in 1986. One of Britain's highest ranking policemen, he was taken off an inquiry into the Royal Ulster Constabulary. It was national news, but nowhere was it covered more fairly or accurately than in the Manchester Evening News.

At a press conference on June 25, 1986 John Stalker resigns as deputy chief constable of Greater Manchester.

Only a few months earlier, in March 1986, John Stalker, on the right, had been greeting the Queen at the Greater Manchester Police Headquarters. The Chief Constable of Greater Manchester, Jim Anderton, is on the left.

BRITAIN'S BIGGEST REGIONAL PAPER

Manchester Evening News

4 o'clock NEWS

37,555   MONDAY, APRIL 2, 1990   CITY FINAL   22p

MAYHEM

ROOF OF REVENGE — prisoners in stocking masks and stolen warders' caps hurl tiles into the courtyard below.

The terror: Pages 2,3, The injured: Pages 4,5, Comment: Page 8, Timetable: Centre Pages

This is the city edition of the newspaper — with deleted copy., which came out on the second day of Strangeways Prison riots. Britain's most serious prison disturbance broke out in the chapel on Sunday, April 1, 1990. By midday 1,000 prisoners were on the loose within the prison, fires were burning in several places and prison staff had withdrawn to secure the perimeter. Most inmates gave themselves up during the first 24 hours and only 120 remained inside by lunchtime on April 2. The events aroused immense public interest and received enormous coverage in the media. Horrific accounts of killings, butchery and torture appeared and, with the information that 20 'body bags' had gone in to the prison, we feared the worst.

The Editor, Michael Unger, offers to act as mediator and is allowed in to the prison to talk to the prisoners who confirm that there are 'no dead.'

The remaining prisoners on the roof of the prison.

No Dead

Prisoners on the roof of the prison, caught in the spotlight of the police helicopter, which continually circled the area. The siege lasted for 25 days.
Picture by Guardian photographer, Denis Thorpe.

In December 1992, IRA Bombs went off in Manchester City centre. Office workers were evacuated from buildings and roads were cordoned off as police received confusing warnings from the terrorists.

These people had just been evacuated from their shops and offices when a second bomb exploded. The shocked and injured are helped by passers-by.

February 1993 — and the mangled wreckage of the gas storage tanks in Warrington after an IRA attack. Police and troops set up road blocks near the site and hunt for clues to the bomb gang.

. . . And, if this was not enough, the town and the whole nation were stunned by the attack on the Warrington shopping centre the following month. Two innocent children died and many were badly injured. Hundreds of Teddy bears and bunches of flowers were left by people to mark the tragedy.

A bright future

The Editor of the Manchester Evening News, Michael Unger who joined the company in 1983.

The following pages are devoted completely to good news, achievement or happy events around Greater Manchester. So, following the bright new image of the 'News' over the last few years, they are recorded in colour.

The first pages show the new technology at Deansgate and Trafford Park — a vast difference to the conditions when Mitchell Henry started his electioneering broadsheet in 1868. We even publish our own weekly colour magazine.

And Manchester is going places once again. It is the heart of a wonderful region with a great deal to be proud of. We were not successful with our British Olympic Bid, but much was achieved. The leader in the Manchester Evening News the following day, September 24, ended with stirring words. — "Victory, it is said, has many fathers; defeat is an orphan. However the defeat at Monte Carlo need not make Manchester a ward of the state.

"Instead, the right to carry Britain's flag — the right we earned by hard work, no little organising skill and a great deal of patient planning — should now make us determined to make Manchester, the shiny city in the north, a beacon of the 21st century as it was for the 19th."

One thing is sure, the "News" will report progress.

The new Manchester Evening News reception area in Spinningfield, off Deansgate, Manchester.

It's an early start for the journalists at the Manchester Evening News — and by 8.45am each day the Editor and his departmental heads are ready to discuss the day's news, pictures, sport and business at the morning conference.

Equipped with the most up-to-date technology, reporters key in their stories to the computer system.

Colour photos flow into our electronic picture desk from all over the world as well as from our staff and freelance photographers.

One of the micro-chip controlled robots delivers a reel of paper to the presses.

A full page sheet is transmitted by a lazer faxing process from the Deansgate offices to Trafford Park.

The paper is printed at the Trafford Park Printers Limited, one of the most modern printing plants in Europe and jointly owned by The Daily Telegraph plc and The Guardian and Manchester Evening News plc.

On the left, an aluminium plate is fitted to one of the Goss web-offset computer controlled presses. Above is the control room and a view of the giant presses.

The pictures sent from Deansgate are received as negatives at Trafford Park.

The papers are collected by the drivers ready for distribution in the distinctive yellow and black vans.

The presses roll and the completed papers are taken by conveyor belt to the publishing room, where they are automatically wrapped in bundles.

The finished product is given a final check. The News prints five editions on weekdays, and at the weekend the Pink sports editions are eagerly bought for their outstanding football, rugby and racing coverage.

NEWSPAPER OF THE YEAR

Manchester Evening News

38,603   **THURSDAY, AUGUST 12, 1993**   30p

PAGES AND PAGES OF JOBS

LYNN MAY'S ADVICE Page 8

WHOOPI & DADDY'S GIRL Page 23

BOB GREAVES COLUMN Page 30

BACK TO FEVER PITCH? Pages 30-31

4 pm

HALF PRICE OR LESS PONTIN'S HOLIDAYS - SEE ENTERTAINMENTS PAGES

Flying doctor Tony leads Brit team

RESCUE DASH TO WAR ZONE

■ TRAINING . . . dad Michael

Toddler in river saved by dad

By Neal Keeling

A DAD'S Army training and "sixth sense" saved his drowning son.

Two-year-old Matthew Barber had sneaked out of his grandma's house, crossed a road and fallen into a river.

His father Michael found him floating on his back motionless, 10ft from the bank with weeds wrapped around his neck.

Michael dived into the Old River near the Boathouse pub at Irlam and carried him to a jetty.

Training

Matthew's mum, Deborah, said: "Michael was in the forces and had medical training. He pushed Matthew's stomach until he coughed up water and started to breath again.

"If Michael had not known what to do, I think we might have lost him.

"The river is a magnet for kids, but there is no fencing and the lifebuoys have been vandalised."

Matthew was back home in Shakespeare Crescent, Eccles, after treatment in the Royal Manchester Children's Hospital.

By Andrew Nott

A TEAM led by Bramhall surgeon Tony Redmond will fly out tonight to help victims of Sarajevo.

Mr Redmond, who formed the now-famous rapid response unit at Withington Hospital, will head for Ancona, Italy.

There, a special centre is to provide immediate help for 41 patients airlifted out of the war zone under Operation Irma, announced by Premier John Major.

Twenty of these will then be brought to Britain and this afternoon St Mary's Hospital in Manchester offered six beds for newly-born babies.

Experienced

Mr Redmond, 41, is Britain's most experienced war-zone and disaster area civilian doctor.

He has set up a second rapid response team at North Staffordshire Royal Infirmary where he now works.

His Sarajevo team has been assembled at top speed though UN executive Peter Kessler said this afternoon that airlifts out of Sarajevo could not start for 48 hours. "Right now our medical team is sweeping across the city," said Mr Kessler. "It's a mammoth undertaking involving local politics at every turn."

After treatment by Mr Redmond's surgeons in Italy, the decision on which child will be

Mother died saving Irma

THE first account emerged today of how tiny Bosnian war victim Irma's mother Elvira died in Sarajevo.

She threw herself on top of the little girl and her sister Medina as a mortar exploded.

Elvira died instantly, Medina survived and Irma was taken to a local hospital with no medicines or hot water.

The condition of Irma, after an operation at a London hospital, was said to be "stable" today. Four surgeons have patched up the five-year-old's intestine, perforated by the mortar blast.

The doctor who treated Irma in Sarajevo said today: "She died once here — she was clinically dead."

But somehow she came back to half-life.

It then took more than a week to get her out, partly because the French doctor heading the local UN medical committee insisted Irma was too ill to be moved.

NOW WE MUST SAVE THEM ALL

First with the News

ON Tuesday the Evening News was the first paper to focus on the plight of ALL the ill children in Sarajevo. Stay ahead of the news with the News.

sent to which hospital in Britain will be taken by Department of Health officials from Whitehall.

The first airlift, from Sarajevo to Ancona, is critical, said a senior Ministry of Defence official.

Bosnian Serbs now pounding the airport with artillery will be given a timetable of RAF jets due to fly in — and hopefully a ceasefire will be arranged.

Meanwhile UN workers in the war zone say treatment should be provided closer to the action. "The sympathy of European countries such as Britian and Sweden is understandable but it makes no sense to fly someone so ill so far away," said one surgeon.

● Rock star The Edge today defended U2's stage show which features a live satellite link with Sarajevo.

He told lunchtime TV that interviews shown at concerts "bring the man in the street to the attention of the world."

■ Comment: Page 6

■ Ready to move: Surgeon Tony Redmond, veteran of battlefield operations

■ WANDERED off . . . Matthew

WEATHER 2 · DIARY 6 · POSTBAG 10 · BMDs 16 · TIME OUT 35 · TV 27-29 · plus 4-PAGE BUSINESS PULLOUT

The design of the Manchester Evening News in August 1993 shows the impact that colour can make to a newspaper. The story is one for us all to be proud of too. Bramhall surgeon, Tony Redmond set up the now famous rapid response unit at Withington Hospital, and formed another such unit at North Staffordshire Royal Infirmary. Mr Redmond is Britain's most experienced war-zone and disaster area civilian doctor, and in August led the British team which flew out to help victims of Sarajevo.

On the right — the crowds gather in Albert Square to see the Christmas lights being switched on in 1992. The giant Father Christmas, illuminated on the tower of the town hall, is once again at the centre of the attractions.

Airport staff celebrate the opening of Terminal 2 at Manchester International Airport with a bottle of champagne.

Train-crazy Samuel Hilton aged four was the first to ride on Ringway's partially completed, Terminal 2 rail link.

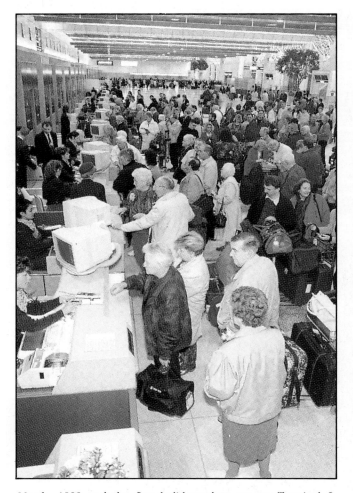

March, 1993 and the first holidaymakers to use Terminal 2 crowd round to check in their luggage.

Rail chiefs Micheal Renshaw, Gordon Jakes and Roger Hill at the airport station of the rail link prior to the opening in 1993.

Guests give a warm welcome to Queen Elizabeth II as she arrives at the Royal Garden Party held in Alexandra Park, Oldham on her visit to the north west in July 1992.

After the opening ceremony of the Metrolink system, the Queen is one of the first passengers on a tram to leave St Peter's Square.

The Queen shares a smile with the people of Manchester on her walkabout when she visited the city in July 1992.

Youngsters from Ordsall with a stilt-walker and uni-cyclist stepped out to mark the opening of a new canalside walkway in Salford. The walkway will eventually link Salford Quays right to the heart of Manchester.

Princesses Beatrice and Eugenie are bridesmaids at the April wedding of their former nanny, Alison Wardley in Withington. *Photographer - John Featherstone.*

Who says that chivalry is dead. A kiss on the hand for Princess Diana during a visit to Manchester in 1991. *Photographer - Mike Grimes.*

The city celebrated with fireworks when it was announced that Manchester was to become the City of Drama for '94.

On January 27, 1992 following the announcement of Manchester's successful bid to be City of Drama 1994, Neil Fountain, Dave Moutrey and Councillor Kath Robinson enjoy a glass of champagne to celebrate.

Cameron Mackintosh brought his hit musical Les Misérables to the Palace Theatre, Manchester, in April 1992 where it played to capacity audiences. The cast pose for a photo-call on stage.

A superb fireworks and light show heralded the completion of the first phase of the Exchange Quay development, Salford in 1992.

Chinatown's famous archway shown at its dramatic best welcomes visitors to an area packed with fabulous restaurants and nightlife.

Announcing the British Olympic Bid for the year 2000 at a press conference in February, 1992 are from left to right, the Duke of Westminster, Bob Scott who is the driving force behind the bid, Graham Stringer, Leader of the City Council, Robert Key, Minister for Manchester and Robert Atkins, Minister for Sport.

The British Olympic Bid team set off to fly to Lausanne to present their hi-tech bid to the International Olympic Committee. Leading the way is 'Manchester' the Olympic Lion mascot, with Bob Scott, Chairman of Manchester 2000, Bill Enevoldson, Finance Director and Frances Toms, Corporate Planning Manager.

Getting set for the World Triathlon Championships on August 22, 1993, Wythenshawe-born European champion sprinter Darren Campbell poses with marathon man Ron Hill who competed in three Olympics.

Sarah Bailey, 14 year old Disley swimming star competed successfully in the Barcelona Paralympics, winning two gold, three silver and two bronze medals. She was also the MEN Sports Personality of the Year for 1992.

Three of our Lancashire cricket stars pose for the camera. From the left Neil Fairbrother, Michael Atherton who captained England in 1993 and Paul Allott.

Niall Quinn on the left with Mike Sheron and David White behind celebrate the Manchester City goal when they draw 1-1 against Manchester United in March 1993.

. . . and Martin Offiah of Wigan Rugby League club celebrates a try in the game against St Helens in the same year.

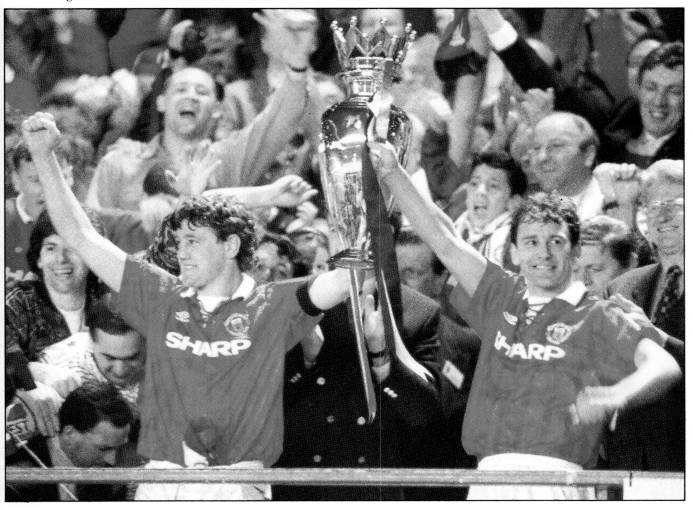

Steve Bruce and captain Bryan Robson of Manchester United with the Premier League Championship Trophy at the end of the season, 1993.

Manchester group Simply Red at Old Trafford. Non stop style from Mick Hucknall.

Now a superstar, Rochdale's Lisa Stansfield in concert at G-Mex.

. . . and show-stoppers Take That — Mark Owen, Jason Orange, Gary Barlow, Robbie Williams and Howard Donald in action before their massed ranks of fans at G-MEX. *Photographer - Bill Batchelor.*

All in a day's work! — The Manchester Evening News provides the backdrop for Greater Manchester Radio presenter, Jeremy Dry's morning show on September 16, 1992. It was the day the bank rate rose 2% - with another 3% threatened, so the pace was hectic, but Jeremy (left) managed to talk to the editor, Michael Unger and, right, news editor Paul Horrocks.

A *final word*

MICHAEL UNGER — EDITOR

Editing the Manchester Evening News is a superb job and I love every minute of it. (You have to get up before 6am every day of the week for 10 years!)

I have an editorial team that is second to none in English journalism.

Day after day we get stories that all the other media follow. (One sometimes think that they would not be able to operate at all if the Evening News didn't come out!).

To maintain this standard, to meet all our deadlines and to give our readers what they want is very demanding, but terribly satisfying. And we all get a particular sense of pleasure when we publish a rewarding exclusive.

Having said that, I, and some of my staff, have tempers that are akin to an Exocet missile and I can be very demanding on my staff. But this particular missile soon returns safely to ground and we get on with the next issue. What this proves is that we have a passion for the paper that is second to none — and without this passion the paper would die.

Laura Davies - 1992 — *Photographer, Tony Cordt*

This book is dedicated to our readers, on whose behalf all Manchester Evening News proceeds will be donated to St Mary's Hospital for mothers and children, Manchester, to aid medical research.

St Mary's is the hospital where Laura was born, and where mothers and children from all over the north west are helped when problems occur before, during and after pregnancy. It is hoped that, by aiding the Paediatric Research Fund, many more children may be helped towards a better quality of life.